Homecare Business Marketing

JULIE JOHNSON RN, MSN

Homecare Business Marketing

Copyright © 2015 by Julie Johnson.

ISBN-13: 978-1511826495

ISBN-10: 1511826495

Printed in the United States of America

"You shall remember the LORD your God, for it is he who gives you power to get wealth…"
Deut 8:18

The first step to

becoming a successful

entrepreneur is to

prepare your mind

-Jane John-Nwankwo

Table of Contents

Chapter One: Unique Characteristics of a Homecare Business

I know that nurses are not only the largest healthcare professionals but are responsible for the delivery of most healthcare, and are often in the best place to be able to see the whole pathway of care.

~Andrew Lansley

Picture it. Your ninety-year-old Aunt Sara is a feisty lady. She has always been your favorite relative. Although she is bright and healthy for her age, lately she has had a couple of falls. You live halfway across the country and you are her only living relative. You have nightmares about finding Sara dead at the bottom of her basement steps. She won't hear of "one of those button gadgets". How can you be sure she is checked on regularly and those jobs she shouldn't be doing alone are covered? How do you know she is taking her medication regularly? Here comes home healthcare.

Your Uncle Andrew, a bachelor, is getting up in years. He frequently forgets to cook for himself and you're pretty sure he doesn't take his medication the way he should. Uncle Andrew needs help to remain—as is his wish—in his own home. There goes home healthcare.

You've just had surgery and are about to be released. Dressings will need to be changed and personal care is not something you can presently do on your own. You want to recuperate in your own home rather than at a convalescent facility.

These and countless other scenarios are instances when home healthcare can help. Home healthcare businesses provide a wide range of health care services that can be given in your home for an illness or injury. Home health care is usually less expensive, more convenient, more comfortable, and just as effective as care you get in a hospital, a skilled nursing facility (SNF), or a convalescent care center.

Home healthcare staff can offer these and other such assistance:

- Wound care for pressure sores or surgical wounds.

- Patient and caregiver training to deal with health-related issues in your home setting
- Intravenous or nutrition therapy.
- Injections.
- Monitoring serious illness and unstable health conditions such as diabetes, cancer, and heart disease.
- Ongoing updates of the status of your health to your family doctor

Home healthcare businesses aim to treat an illness or injury. Home health care helps you get better, maintain as much independence as possible, regain your independence, and become as self-sufficient as possible.

From a home healthcare business, it is realistic to expect the following assistance:

- Doctor's orders are needed to start care. Once your doctor refers you for home health services, the home health agency will schedule an appointment and come to your home to talk to you about your needs and ask you some questions about your health.

- The home health agency staff will also talk to your doctor about your care and keep your doctor updated about your progress.

- It's important that home health staff see you as often as the doctor ordered

• Home healthcare is less hassle for clients and their relatives as it is delivered in the comfort of the client's home.

• Easier for family and friends to visit and to accommodate their loved ones routines and lifestyle.

• Home healthcare promotes healing and provides more safety from infections because clients are not exposed to others who may be carrying germs, illnesses and infections.

• Home healthcare allows more freedom and independence for clients, their families and their caregivers like pharmacist, physiotherapist, general practitioner and specialists.

• Home healthcare is more affordable than inpatient care for individuals, their families and the community taxpayers.

• Home healthcare is tailored to meet the needs of each individual patient.

• Home healthcare reduces re-hospitalization because clients are monitored closely, kept away from infectious environments, and their family doctor is given ongoing reports of their condition. In this way potential problems can be addressed quickly keeping clients' health from deterioration.

As efficient and skilled as they are, home healthcare businesses are not set up for—nor qualified to deal with—every client need. Home healthcare businesses should be expected to do the all following tasks:

- Check your blood pressure, temperature, heart rate, and breathing.

- Check to see what you are eating and drinking.

- Check that you're taking your prescription and other drugs.

- Make sure you are doing follow-up treatments correctly.

- Ask about your pain level.

- Check safety and security in your home.

- Teach self-care skills.

- Coordinate your care schedules with other caregivers such as physiotherapy, occupational therapy, speech and language therapy. This means they must communicate regularly with you, your doctor, and anyone else who gives you care.

As the average age of North Americans increases, facilities that specialize in eldercare become more numerous, more varied and more critical. Before we look at how to market a homecare business, let's investigate what makes a homecare business unique.

When life changes due to an illness, accident or aging, one of the biggest concerns facing individuals and their families is how the client can maintain independence and personal care. Clients often need assistance with grocery shopping, doing errands, attending doctor's and other healthcare appointments, reminders and organization of their medication schedule, meal planning and preparation, laundry, and housekeeping.

What is a Homecare Business?

Home healthcare is a system of care provided by skilled practitioners to clients in their homes. There is non-medical home care and medical home care, usually referred to as home healthcare. The non-medical home care basically offers companion care services, while home health care provides medical care like physical therapists, nurses, etc. Home Healthcare businesses operate in conjunction and under the direction of a physician. Home healthcare businesses are prepared to provide whatever is needed: nursing care, physical, occupational, speech-language therapy and/or medical social services.

Homecare businesses are dedicated to helping clients improve function and live with greater independence. Homecare businesses promote the client's highest possible well-being. They are committed to helping clients who wish to do so to remain at home, to avoid hospitalization or admission to long-term care facilities.

Who Refers?

Physicians or other institutions like CCAS or hospital social workers often collaborate to make a referral for homecare. Individuals or their families may also make a referral.

Homecare businesses provide these services, relieving stress from clients and their families. The care provided by a qualified, professional homecare business is often an ideal option.

Homecare Business Setting

The home healthcare setting is different from hospitals and other institutional environments. In the home healthcare businesses caregivers work alone in the clients' homes. Other support service providers are available as needed either in the home or in a clinic, office, or hospital setting.

Caregivers have less direct contact with physicians than in hospital settings. The doctor relies on the caregiver to make assessments and report changes.

Home healthcare providers spend more time on paperwork than hospital nurses. They also have to deal with reimbursement concerns.

Other concerns in the homecare business workplace setting include: patient safety and quality of outcomes, the degree of patient autonomy in the home, limited supervision of caregivers by medical and business staff and situational variables unique to each client environment all make the homecare business challenging and flexible.

Homecare business is a scalable service designed to provide exactly the needed amount and type of care for each client. Not all homecare businesses — or the clients they serve — are the same. However, homecare businesses can be expected to provide these options:

1. **In-Home Needs Assessment**

   An in-home assessment should be provided by a physiotherapist, an occupational therapist and/or a registered nurse. The idea is to ensure that such areas as medical issues, personal needs and wishes are investigated by a trained professional(s) who assess(es) the client in their own home.

2. **Homecare Professional Qualifications**

   When one employs a homecare business, clients expect to receive quality care from a sensitive, empathetic, and caring person. Homecare businesses do background checks to ensure their caregivers are reliable and honest. They do employment verification checks, check references, and verify credentials. As well, ongoing assessments are conducted and regular meetings are held with clients and/or their families.

3. Experienced Employees

Good homecare businesses strive to hire only experienced caregivers. Caregivers who have experience attending to the needs of clients are an advantage for both client and the business. Their knowledge and expertise put them in a group ready and proven to meet client needs right from the outset.

4. Competency Assessment of Employees

A good homecare business tests its employees on an ongoing basis to ensure personal health, skills, and techniques. Standard TB Testing, drug testing are standard procedures.

5. Code of Conduct

Homecare businesses must ensure their employees operate within the guidelines, training and certification program developed to enhance caregivers' skills in areas of social and client interaction.

6. Attendance

One of the most serious problems of a caregiver business is non-attendance of the caregiver in the client's home. Homecare businesses use creative ways to reward and encourage perfect attendance.

7. Supervision and Random Visits

Good homecare businesses have plans for supervision of their employees including unscheduled visits to clients' homes. Field nurse supervisors' visits ensure clients are receiving the best care. Clients are given a chance to communicate any concerns that might be uncomfortable to discuss with a caregiver.

8. Ongoing, Scheduled Dialogue

Good homecare businesses have a process to keep clients and/or families informed. Caregivers in good homecare businesses keep careful notes of each visit to, thus, provide an overview of homecare patient activities. These are always available. In addition, caregivers should be trained to alert family members of changes or concerns. Effective communication is a two-way street.

9. Flexible Scheduling and Overtime Policy

Unexpected problems arise. Needs change. Thus, a good homecare business needs to have a clearly stated and transparent policy to address these changes.

10. Full-Service Business

Needs of clients vary and often change over time. A good homecare business is ready and willing to provide services for all client needs. These might include personal hygiene care, physiotherapy, errands, light housekeeping, medical procedures, post-operative care, nursing services, and rehabilitative therapy.

Benefits for the Client of Having Home Health Care

First and foremost home health care allows patients to receive personal care in the privacy and comfort of their homes. For aging and homebound individuals, in-home care allows people who wish to do so to be as functional and independent as possible. This gives them a much greater sense of security and dignity. Receiving home health care helps reduce the likelihood of readmissions to the hospital. Research has shown that patients recuperating from illness, injury, or surgical procedures heal more quickly and more successfully when recovering at home versus in a medical facility.

A primary aim of medical care is ensuring that clients who are ill, elderly, or have mobility issues get high quality, personal, and medical care. Home health care is designed to meet these needs. It provides compassionate, personalized service in the convenience and comfort of the client's home.

Primary Benefits to the Client

• Home health care is provided in the comfort of the patient's home
• This arrangement makes it easier for family and friends to visit and interact naturally
• Promotes healing and provides more safety from infections
• Allows more freedom and independence
• More affordable than inpatient care
• Tailored to the needs of each individual patient
• Reduces re-hospitalizations

What are the Unique Marketing Problems of a Home Healthcare Business?

Home healthcare businesses are not like other businesses. Often the referral person/business is not the individual who is the direct client. So there is a "middle man" so to speak. This middle man or group or business may be the one who is your target market. People who suggest or select a home healthcare business include: other health care professionals such as physicians, physiotherapists, occupational therapists or speech therapist. Referring businesses might also include: attorneys, insurance companies and health care rehabilitation businesses or institutions.

There is also a high degree of probability that the "client" is the family of the patient or person who you serve. This primary client may have had little or nothing to do with the selection of a homecare business. Thus, home healthcare businesses have all these niche markets.

Home healthcare businesses have to market to a wide "first referrals" group. This widely varied group includes people involved in medicine, law, social services and insurance companies. In addition, marketing also has to appeal to the consumer: those individuals and families in need of home health care and/or social services.

Marketing presentations also need to consider members of the community their home healthcare business serves as these people may be potential clients and future clients.

With such a large group in the target market for a home healthcare business, marketing campaigns must be varied and specific. Your home healthcare business needs to appeal to the primary user. In addition, if it is to be successful financially it must target the people who will be handling the referrals. In *Home Healthcare and Hospice Industry Blog,* Bobbie Robertson makes these suggestions for increasing referrals to your home healthcare business:

1. Create a list of the top referral sources in your physical and professional market area. Be sure to include: doctors, social workers, in-hospital professionals, private physiotherapy and occupational therapy businesses, insurance companies, other healthcare agencies, extended care facilities, community outreach groups, senior centers...

2. Devise a contest or recognition night event to award the top healthcare sales professional in the area. Include both a form of recognition and a prize. This "awards event" accomplishes two things: It focuses on people and businesses that have given you referrals and the event garners publicity for your business.

3. Visit each of your frequent referral sources to tell them about a recognition event you are planning. Ask them to nominate one, two or three individuals or agencies from the ones they have worked with the most often. Host an event—luncheon or

dinner—to thank both the referral sources and their nominees. This is a way to get known in your business, recognize those who refer and get public exposure for both your business and the people/groups that refer your business to others. It provides community awareness that your business exists.

4. If you are hiring a marketing professional who knows the home healthcare business.

   It is important to have public exposure in the home healthcare business where referrals are so vital.

   Your business needs a message to communicate to your referral source. They need to know why they should refer to your home healthcare business over all the others out there.

Home healthcare businesses have good service provided by competent staff. So why refer to your over any others? Physicians will refer to you because they believe you provide great care to their patients. Service and outcomes motivate patients and referral sources and give them a reason to prefer your agency. Marketing effectively gives your business that extra hook that will make referrals come your way rather than go to the competition. Finding that hook and making it work for your home healthcare business is what good marketing is all about!

In the next chapter we'll talk about why marketing is so important and how to make sure your marketing is directed toward the right target audience.

What are the Rewards of Owning a Home Healthcare Business?

Whether B2B or B2C, I believe passionately that good marketing essentials are the same.

We all are emotional beings looking for relevance, context and connection

~Beth Comstock

1. You are a Caregiver

> You are in a job where others depend on you and where you reap the rewards of their trust and gratitude.

2.Others Value what You Do

Gratitude for what you do comes from family, friends and neighbors of the clients you serve. You and your business are held in high esteem by the community you serve. Others look up to you for the job you do.

3.You are in Control

600,000 new businesses are founded each year in America each year. Why?

Many entrepreneurs are "Type-A" personalities who like to take control and make decisions. Owning your own home healthcare business allows you to shape its culture. You are making the decisions on how best to steer your company and to meet the needs of your clients. When you are able to make your own decisions about how best to achieve your goals it is highly rewarding.

4.Work/Life Balance

One of the most cited benefits of owning your own home healthcare business is flexibility. You can shape your work hours to fit your clients' needs and still find time to spend with your family.

5.You Get to Associate with Some Awesome People

People involved in the care of others are selfless and resilient. What a great work environment! Service providers associated with home healthcare include: doctors, nurses, physiotherapists, occupational therapists, and psychologists.

6.You can shape the Culture of Your Work Environment When you work for someone else, you almost never choose your colleagues and certainly never your supervisors. If you don't like your co-workers or your boss, your only alternative as an employee is to start sending those resumes. When you own your own business, you get to make the decisions about who to hire (and fire). You get the opportunity to surround yourself with positive people. These employees and clients give you confidence and optimism.

7.You   Reap   the   Rewards

Of course owning your own home healthcare business comes with risks and worries. But, with those risks come rewards. You learn to create exit strategies for bad situations and how to maximize good ones. There is exhilaration in working on a shared project with a team of enthusiastic professionals, overcoming all of the obstacles, and seeing the fruits of your labor.

8. Ownership Offers Challenges

A home healthcare business offers lots of challenges and variations different from a routine job where you are performing the same tasks day after day—for years. Instead, your days will be filled with new challenges each day. You will rarely experience the same day twice. You will learn new information and acquire new talents. Ownership is a lifelong learning experience. Needs change. Technology changes. You are always finding better ways to run your business and serve clients.

9. You Get to Pursue Your Passion

Even though there will be long hours in the home healthcare business, it won't feel like work. You will have fun doing it. You will enjoy the satisfaction of promoting and supporting something you truly believe in.

10.You're Part of a Network
Working in the home healthcare business affords you the opportunity to network with others in your community and farther afield who are affiliated with offering home healthcare services. This broadens your horizons and offers divergent ideas and innovations for your business.

11.You avoid the Frustrations of Red Tape

Small business owners are eager to get things done. They get creative about avoiding red tape that slows things down and throws up road blocks for worthy and time-sensitive projects. As the owner of a small business, you can react quicker than big companies. Your home healthcare business has the flexibility to be proactive, to run with new ideas and to be at the forefront of home healthcare products, techniques, services, or promotional strategies. Owning your own home healthcare business lets you be proactive rather than reactive.

12. You Can Connect With Your Clients

When you own your own home healthcare business you can interact with your clients. You can be front line rather than getting caught up in layers of bureaucracy and automated greetings.

Small business owners thrive on dealing face to face with clients. You also have the decision about which clients and types of clients you serve– and don't serve.

13. Giving Back to the Community

When you run a home healthcare business you are most assuredly giving back to the community or communities where you operate. You can feel proud that you are creating innovative ways for your clients to remain in their home with your support. Within that community you can offer useful products and services donate to charities, support community causes and solve problems others. As a business owner you also create opportunities for people to do fulfilling jobs they love.

14. Feeling of Pride and Self-Worth

One of the biggest differences in owning your own company as opposed to working for someone else is the sense of pride and self-worth. Your home healthcare is the fruits of your labor. You've built something of your own. You can feel justifiable pride. This is self-actualization. People are interested in what you've done, why you chose this field, and how your business continues to grow and prosper. You are a role model and inspiration to others.

15. Opportunities to Mentor Other Entrepreneurs

One of the most rewarding contributions you can make is serving as a mentor to eager entrepreneurs just starting out. They may be entering a healthcare field or something totally unrelated. Nevertheless, you have marketing skills and business expertise to offer. Your involvement may be as formal as serving as part of a community mentoring program like Junior Achievement or Young Entrepreneurs. It might be as casual as offering to help a colleague or being asked to help. No matter which the arrangement is, mentoring is a win-win situation. Your skills and ideas will blossom and grow as you help others.

Chapter Two: Why Worry about Marketing?

Our jobs as marketers are to understand how the customer wants to buy and help them do so. ~Bryan Eisenberg

What is Marketing?

Marketing is the process by which goods and services move from an idea to clients or customers. Think of marketing as everything a business does to build a relationship between your home healthcare business and the consumer or client.

At its simplest level marketing involves creating or locating a product or service needed in the area you serve, finding a niche market for your product or service and working you magic. That means put your product or service on sale in a location the people you know want your product visit regularly. Marketing also involves pricing your goods or services at a level those who want/need your services or goods will be prepared to buy.

Marketing is based on thinking about your home healthcare business in terms of satisfying customer needs. Marketing differs from selling because in that selling concerns itself with the tricks and techniques of getting people to exchange their cash for your goods or services. Marketing is concerned with the values that the exchange is all about.

Marketing views your business process as a tightly integrated effort to discover, create, arouse and satisfy customer needs. Marketing has less to do with getting customers to pay for your product. It has more to do with developing a demand for your product or service and fulfilling the client's needs.

What is Involved in Marketing?

(1) Identification, selection and development of a product or service

(2) Determination of its the price the market will pay for this product or service

(3) Selection of a distribution channel to reach the customer or client

(4) Development and implementation of a promotional strategy to convince clients to purchase this good or service.

The Four P's of Marketing

Understanding marketing involves defining four elements:

1. Products and/or Services

- What does the customer want?
- How will your product or service satisfy the clients' needs?
- What features does your product or service have to meet these needs?
  - What features does your service fail to meet?
  - What costly features of your service will your clients likely not even need or use?
- How and where will your prospective clients use your home healthcare service?
- What are the unique features of your service that will appeal to clients?

- What is it to be called?

- How is it branded?

- How is it differentiated versus your competitors?

- What is the most it can cost to provide, and still be sold sufficiently profitably?

2. **Place**

   - Where can your prospective clients expect to find information about your services?

   - Do you have an online presence?

   - Is the information attractive, informative, and user-friendly?

   - Is there a clear link from the information site to finding you?

   - Do you have a clear, effective follow up procedure for queries?

3. **Price**

- What is the value of your service to the client?

- Are there established price points for home healthcare services in this area?

- Is the client price sensitive?

- Will a small decrease in price gain you extra market share? Or will a small increase be indiscernible, and so gain you extra profit margin?

- What discounts should be offered to trade customers, or to other specific segments of your market?

- How does your pricing compare to the competitive businesses in your geographic area?

4. Promotion

- In what places and when can you get across your marketing messages to your target market? Have you considered many varied and unusual platforms for promoting your home healthcare business?

- Will you reach your audience by advertising in the press, or on TV, or radio, or on billboards? By using direct marketing mailshot? Through PR? On the Internet?

- When is the best time to promote your home healthcare business? Is there seasonality in the market? Are there any personal, client, environmental or other issues that suggest or dictate the timing of your market launch?

- What considerations affect the timing of subsequent promotions?

- How does your competition market? What effect do their choices have on your decisions to market and how you will market?

- How do community factors influence your choice of promotional activity?

- What other issues do you need to consider when promoting your home healthcare business?

Why is Marketing Important for Your Home Healthcare Business?

Marketing is the very heart of your business success. Almost all other aspects of your business depend on its successful marketing. The overall marketing umbrella covers advertising, public relations, promotions and sales. Marketing is a process by which a product or service is introduced and promoted to potential customers. Without marketing, your business may offer the best products or services in your industry, but none of your potential customers would know about it. Without marketing, sales may crash and companies may have to close.

Whether you're operating an established home healthcare business or starting a new home healthcare business venture, a successful marketing strategy is important to your success.

A good marketing plan accomplishes several goals:

It builds a stronger, more consistent image for your business.

It increases the faith and loyalty your clients and your community have for your business.

It makes the general public more aware of your business and the services it offers.

It reinforces with your community, your clients, and your supporters that your brand and service has value.

It builds a networking base within the community.

It helps your home healthcare business attract and retain the best employees.

Mistakes in Marketing

Microsoft Business website states that many small businesses make the mistake of viewing marketing as something you don't need to do or you need do only from time to time. For marketing to be effective, you must have a continuous marketing plan that targets a niche market in order to ensure the ongoing success of your home healthcare business.

Some businesses think they don't need to market. They are established in their community and count on word of mouth to do their advertising. That's all fine when times are good and competition is low. By the time these businesses realize they need to market it is often too late.

Some businesses refuse to recognize that times have changed and they should too. Social media is a classic example. Those who do not use it are overlooking an inexpensive and highly effective marketing tool.

Some companies do not accurately identify or address their niche market. This mistake can be instant and deadly.

Failure to respond to feedback is another deadly mistake—particularly in this age of social media. What these businesses that neglect to provide feedback fail to realize is that social media is all about connections.

Getting the Word out

For a home healthcare business to succeed, the potential clients must be aware of the services it offers.

Unless your business is known in the niche market and the community and you have reached your customers directly, you need marketing strategies to create an awareness. Without marketing, your potential clients may never become aware of the services your business provides. Your business may not be given the opportunity to serve these potential clients.

Using marketing to promote your home healthcare business gives your company a chance to offer your services to prospective customers. It gets your business on the radar of your niche market.

Increasing Referrals and Revenue

Once your home healthcare business gets on the radar screen of your potential clients, it increases your chances that referrals and clients will use your services.

As awareness becomes a reality, new customers start to tell friends and family about your services. Your referrals will steadily increase as the word spreads. Marketing strategies start the ball rolling.

Business Credibility

The success of a home healthcare business rests on its solid reputation. Marketing builds brand name recognition and tells the community about the services you provide. Marketing makes your company name a household word. When your home healthcare business achieves the high expectations of the public, its reputation is solid. As your company's reputation grows, your business expands and your referrals and bottom line increase. The reputation of your home healthcare business is built through active participation in community programs, effective communication, and quality services. These are created or supported by marketing initiatives.

Beating the Competition

Marketing also fosters a healthy completion in the community. Marketing efforts get the word out on your services so it reaches the intended consumers, and also other home healthcare businesses competing for the same niche market. This means clients seeking home healthcare have the benefit of a range of home healthcare businesses offering a wide variety of services and competitive prices for those services.

Without competition, home healthcare businesses might have a monopoly. They could charge whatever they wanted. Moreover, new home healthcare businesses wouldn't stand a chance of ever becoming successful. Marketing facilitates the healthy competition. Small businesses and new businesses get a chance to thrive in a level-field marketplace.

Marketing Considerations

Marketing can be very expensive. In getting the world out, a startup home healthcare business might have to spend up to half of its net profits on marketing programs. The following year, your marketing budget might drop to 30 percent of your net profits. A good marketing program is one that gives your company the best chance of success by using a healthy mix of different forms of marketing including: website development, public relations, print and broadcast advertising, design and printing for all print materials, trade shows and other special events.

Highly Effective Marketing Practices

1. **Good Marketers Find out what Potential Clients Want**

Good marketers do not assume they can diagnose the needs of your potential clients merely by guessing. They do thorough investigations via polls, calls, discussions and/or research into what you provide and the services your niche market wants and needs.

45

Having learned this information marketing staff begins to fashion a marketing plan to appeal to your target market.

2. Good Marketers Tell a Story

Good marketers work at making connections between your home healthcare business and the community it serves. The marketing solution arises from the problems your service will address. Keeping dialogue open and ongoing is key to selling your services. Potential clients and referral agencies do not care about your services. What they care about is how your services can help their loved one retain independence or help a patient thrive. The direct service receiver or client cares about himself and how you can meet his needs. Good marketers demonstrate that they hear these needs and can address them.

3. Good Marketers Build Relationships

A good marketing program aims at building trust between your home healthcare business and the potential clients it will serve. Great marketers aim at building relationship whose foundation is admiration and credibility. You want your clients to see you not just as a business person but first and foremost as someone who cares about them and will stop at nothing to ensure their comfort and safety are met. Good marketing builds a relationship between you and your client.

4. Good Marketers Earn You the Right to Offer Your Services

Good marketers earn you respect. Their campaign is aimed at gaining clients' desire to know you and your wonderful services better.

5. Good Marketers See Everything as a Hurdle

In today's fast-paced, multi-option world, good marketers see everything as a challenge. It is their job to get your "foot in the door". Good marketers make inroads for you. They pave the way to introductions. Great marketers look for facts and data that enable them to make incremental improvements. Good marketers know the real goal of marketing is to focus on the long-term strategies to get customers.

6. Good Marketers Know their Niche Market

Successful marketers choose a niche market carefully and stick to it. They use their considerable experience, knowledge, theories and ideas to create content around it. They deliver BITE SIZE CHUNKS of information aimed at getting their audience to take action. Outstanding niche marketing minimizes misunderstanding and delivers high value information that aims to make a visitor a client.

How Effective is Marketing?

Because the purpose of business is to create a customer, the business enterprise has two – and only two – basic functions: marketing and innovation. Marketing and innovation produce results; all the rest are costs.
~Peter Drucker

Since marketing represents a huge expenditure in both money and time, you want to know you are getting your money's worth! Consider these facts:

- Businesses that pro-actively communicate prosper; business that don't tend to fail. Communication is essential to creating a brand.

- Branding result from interacting with a brand—much of which is created as a marketing tool. Clever brands don't happen entirely by accident. Behind every successful company is a successful brand. Behind every successful brand is a good marketer who has asked the critical question: "What makes this home healthcare business different from the rest?"

- Coca-Cola—one of the world's most recognized brands—spends billions annually on marketing efforts. Coca-Cola knows exactly what those dollars will bring them.

- Start-up businesses—whether online or bricks-and-mortar venture—regard marketing as a means of survival.

- Companies make the mistake of seeing marketing as medicine to "fix" a sick company. They should see it as food to make sure that company stays healthy. Unfortunately by the time they realize their mistake, it is too late to save the company!

- Continuous marketing prevents "reputation rot". Instead of dated or inaccurate information, your target market has recent, correct information about your home healthcare business.

- With an effective integrated marketing plan, your home healthcare business has a comprehensive, integrated marketing plan. You can communicate such things as: your company's mission, values and messages in the most effective way for your target audience.

- Ongoing marketing targets new potential clients as your company evolves. Marketing assesses your target and adjusts the message and/or strategies or visuals as needed.

- Ongoing marketing provides options. Active marketing, there should always be more demand for your offering than you can actually meet. This gives you the option to pick and choose your potential clients focusing on options which bring in the most revenue.

- Ongoing marketing ensures your business' future. Active, ongoing marketing secures your company's future by creating business. Smart business owners know that times change and healthy businesses can hit lean times. Marketing plants the seeds for future business.

Successful marketing helps a home healthcare business go beyond the "me too" level to create a compelling brand experience. Unless you have a clear technology, service or cost-based advantage, you need to come up with something that is different. That's what good marketing does.

How Does Marketing Differ from Advertising?

Advertising is only a part of a marketing program. Marketing also includes:

- Communication

- Community Involvement

- Customer Relations

- Distribution

- Media Planning

- Marketing Research and Development

- Pricing

- Product/Services Promotion

- Sales

In the next chapter we will look at marketing techniques which are effective for home healthcare businesses.

Chapter Three: Homecare Marketing Strategies

Marketing is not only much broader than selling; it is not a specialized activity at all. It encompasses the entire business. It is the whole business seen from the point of view of its final result, that is from the customer's point of view. Concern and responsibility for marketing must therefore permeate all areas of the enterprise.
~Peter Drucker

What is a Marketing Strategy?

A *marketing strategy* is an initiative or plan or technique to increase referrals, profits and/or to achieve a competitive advantage over others in the same business.

What is Included in Marketing Strategy?

Marketing strategy includes both basic and long-term activities that deal with the analysis of your strategic situation of your home healthcare business and the formulation, evaluation and selection of market strategies and contribute to your company's marketing objectives or goals. Marketing strategy is aimed at one of two areas: Innovation and growth.

Innovation Strategies

Innovation strategies focus on your business' creation and introduction of a new product or service designed to improve the quality of life of the clients you serve.

Innovation strategies include:

A: Pioneers:

Pioneer marketing focuses on being first to offer a product or service. This marketing strategy ponders the following questions:

- Does it pay to be first with a service?
- Is being a pioneer worth the risk?
- Is it better to wait and learn from the experiences of the first entrant to the market?
- What is the proper balance between the risks and rewards?
- If you are a pioneer, what can you do to prevent share erosion when a new player enters the market?
- If you are a late entrant, what strategies should you adopt to make your entry successful?

Studies show that in most cases, being first to the market provides a significant and sustained market-share advantage over later entrants. Still, later entrants can succeed by adopting distinctive positioning and marketing strategies. Pioneers in most industries, once they have reached the status of incumbent, are powerful. Sometimes, however, they get complacent or are not in a position to cater to the growing or shifting demands of the marketplace. New entrants can take advantage of gaps in the offerings of these aging pioneers, or find innovative ways to market their product or service.

Pioneers with a distinctive presence in the marketplace need to be in a position to react, or even better, anticipate potential entrants and increase the barriers to their entry.

For example, a pioneer may be in a position to reduce its price and decrease the value of the business for a new entrant, or it can block entrance entirely by controlling key distribution channels.

Competitive strategies include:

1.Reducing the price of your home healthcare services to penetrate an existing market. By introducing your healthcare services at a lower price than that being charged by the pioneer, as a latecomer, you can attract new clients who might not have chosen home healthcare as an option because it would have been too expensive for them to consider it. Reducing the price can also convince some of the pioneer's present clients to over to your home healthcare business. Warning: reducing the price as a marketing strategy is likely to produce two negative outcomes: The pioneer will be prepared not to be collegial and your bottom line will not be as healthy because you cut your prices.

2.Improving your service to appeal to your niche market. Home healthcare businesses can compete by being innovative in a major minor way. An incremental innovation might be an enhanced version of a service you are already providing. This incremental innovation might serve to attract a smaller segment of the target market or to attract new clients outside the target market. This service can complement or replace options available to current clients. A radical change might be a service you've never before provided. It may serve to target new clients or widen the service to existing clients.

An example of an incremental innovation might be wheelchair exercises to add to the present exercise or Zumba aquatics to replace the current water exercise program. A radical innovation might be adding computer skills classes where none existed previously.

2.Targeting a new geographic market for existing services is another competitive marketing strategy. Businesses often look to extend their area as their business grows and they seek more lucrative markets. As a home healthcare business, you might look at other nearby physical areas where there is a high concentration of older potential clients.

3.Developing new ways to access new markets or better penetrate the existing ones is also a competitive marketing strategy. Your business might consider

global or simply setting up a home healthcare business in a nearby town or community. There is a risk that the cash required to reach other geographic markets may not be worth the cost and time. Focusing on your present market area, where your company has a good rapport with the community can be safer and bring quicker successes. Developing new ways to reach the present area market might be accomplished through new marketing strategies, improved advertising, repackaging your services…A good example would be using social media avenues to reach the target market in your area.

While effective it must be remembered that Pioneer marketing strategy costs the most because:

> 1) the product or service innovation necessitates a higher investment in research and development than product or service imitation does.

2) the pioneer must incur heavy expenditure on necessary marketplace education and testing, advertising, and promotion. Those who follow reap the benefits of the pioneer's labor.

Even when these considerations have been factored in, companies like Hewlett-Packard and 3M know that pioneer marketing strategies have made more than 60 percent of their revenues in the past three years. These companies have succeeded in pioneering at a very high level.

Even when close followers try to grab a slice of business or create niche strategies to compete, pioneers can maintain their competitive advantage. Possession is nine points of the law. Pioneers can:

1) increase entrance barriers for later entrants.

2) be innovative faster than latecomers.

3) build a market-responsive business.

Pioneers have incomplete information. But, they can take advantage of this by using effective signaling mechanisms to block later competition. Pioneers can cut price to deter potential new entrants. New entrants usually focus on a few key segments of the market. It is important for pioneers to understand their end-user client and adopt a differential pricing schedule that's attractive to this niche market. Pioneers can also lock up key distribution channels. This makes it hard for new entrants to gain access to the market.

Pioneers can also offer special, enhanced customer service packages or customer loyalty rewards making it harder for the completion to pierce the market.

B: Close Followers

Close followers, as the name suggests, are early or second followers of pioneers. Why is this marketing trend successful?

1. Close followers reap the benefits of costly research and development of pioneers.

2. People are by nature cautious. With pioneers they often assume a "wait and see" strategy. By the time close followers have their product or service on the scene the cautious buyers are ready to buy. The worth of the product or service has been proven by the pioneers.

3. Close followers can afford to be price competitive because they do not have to cover research and development expenses.

C: Late Followers

Late entrants or late followers at first glance would seem to have no advantages. However, there are some things to keep in mind:

Later entrants or late followers can differentiate themselves markedly in potential clients' views.

Late entrants can make substantial changes to the healthcare service and/or to how it is promoted. New advertising might appeal to a different age group or clients' different needs.

A second way late followers might market is by finding creative new ways to increase service.
A study has discovered that the market-share advantage for the early entrants is from higher trial penetration.
Sample-service or free trial is effective. Potential clients are offered a "free week-end" of home healthcare service, for example.
Later entrants can also split the already established businesses by focusing on a specific service or target market.

Later followers can position themselves using special enhancers like added services or an extra week free or thirteen months for the price of twelve.

Later entrants can succeed by pursuing a new or fast-growing niche market like a new seniors' apartment building or a new hospital. Such shifts in the niche market can often prove beneficial to the late follower who does not already have a caseload to keep happy while pursuing a new target audience.

Late followers can often achieve success by pursuing clients who are well off and willing to pay a higher price for a home healthcare business that focuses on wealthier clientele, offering services geared to this specific market.

Growth Strategies

Growth strategies are aimed at increasing the area of your business, expanding, taking on more clients, hiring more staff…

Horizontal growth focuses on acquiring other home healthcare businesses in the same geographic area.

Vertical growth or can be either forward growth or backward growth. In forward integration your home healthcare business grows towards its clients. This might include adding outreach offices or having more services delivered right within the client's home.

In backward growth or integration your home healthcare business grows towards its source of referral. For example: you might set your business' office in a medical center or near a hospital or extended care facility.

Diversification

Diversification is a marketing strategy in which your home healthcare business is creating a new service for that new market. This is the riskiest marketing strategy because your business has no experience in the new market and does not know if the service is going to be successful with this target market.

Intensification

Intensification refers to growth by working with your current home healthcare businesses more vigorously. There are three ways in which you might use intensification as a marketing strategy:

1. Market Penetration

Market penetration refers to concentrating on your current home healthcare business and directing resources and efforts to making your service grow within its target market and geographic community.

2. Marketing Development

Marketing development consists of selling your existing services to new customers in related market areas by adding different ways of serving your clients or by changing the way your services are advertised or promoted in the media.

3. Services Development

Services development involves noticeable modification of existing services or the creation of new but related services that can be marketed to present clients through established channels.

Chapter Four: How to Get Hospital Referrals

What are Hospital Referrals?

Hospital referrals are not like "word of mouth" or "telephone" referrals. Hospital referrals are part of a specific referral system. Hospital referrals are part of a methodically process that your business has worked to get set in place. Hospital referrals are aimed at enticing qualified prospects through your association with decision makers in the hospital setting.

Hospital referrals are clients leaving hospital but still requiring convalescent or rehabilitation care. Clients may also be leaving hospital for long-term senior care. This is a growing and lucrative niche market for any home healthcare business.

Clients leaving hospital who are not candidates or are reluctant to accept placement in an extended care facility often require extensive and/or intensive support of a home healthcare business.

The trend presently is to consider a home placement at least until this proves not to be sufficient support or until needs change and it is no longer feasible to deliver services within the client's home.

In order to get hospital referrals it is advantageous to build relationships with physicians and social workers. These are often front line referring agents.

Why are Hospital Referrals Important?

Research shows that nearly half of home healthcare business is generated through referrals. When you are in the home healthcare business, marketing to hospitals is a lucrative business.

Chances are many of your clients have been hospitalized for surgery, a fall, an injury, physiotherapy or other convalescent care service. As they make the transition to their homes — or to a rehabilitation facility — they will need support. That's where your home healthcare business comes in.

How Can You Garner Referrals?

There are as many ways to get hospital referrals for your home healthcare business as there are home healthcare business owners. The trick is to be creative and to know your audience.

1. Provide Quality Service

The first step is to provide the best quality of service it is within your power to give your clients. When decision makers refer others to your home healthcare business, they are putting their reputation on the line too. They want to receive positive feedback. If they do not get it, they are unlikely to continue to refer clients to your service.

2. Develop a Good Referral Requesting Attitude

Being good at asking for referrals requires that you know about your service and how it helps people. You must believe in the service you offer and be able to articulate convincingly why your service is the one the decision makers should choose. If you are unable to do this, learn how. Practice. Watch others. Take a course. Sign up for a workshop. Referral systems are that important!

3. **Educate Your Potential Referees**

   There are dozens of ways to do this: videos, facility come and go events, testimonials...You are limited only by your imagination! If decision makers are expected to send you referrals they need to know what services you provide, how your facility is set up and how it compares to the competition.

4. **Drop in**

As a strategy there is nothing wrong with "dropping in" when you are in the vicinity. You may actually get lucky and find a physician or other decision maker who has the time—and interest—in talking to you. Dropping in works more effectively if you've already had referrals from this individual and the two of you have established a relationship. Otherwise, it is a lot more effective to schedule an appointment or make contact in another manner. Generally the decision makers are too busy and/or too protective of their precious time to look favourably upon a drop in.

Whether "dropping in" works depends upon those you hope to talk to and what it is you are trying to accomplish. If you are seeking information "dropping in" may work. Whether "dropping in" works depends upon those you hope to talk to and what it is you are trying to accomplish. If you are seeking information "dropping in" may work. If you want to remind the physician and his staff of your existence and put a face to a name then just "popping in" may be useful.

Whether "dropping in" works depends upon those you hope to talk to and what it is you are trying to accomplish. If you are seeking information "dropping in" may work. If you want to remind the physician and his staff of your existence and put a face to a name then just "popping in" may be useful. If you are trying to develop a relationship leading to referrals, you may fall flat. That said: There may be times when "stopping by" may well result in a referral.

5. Liaison

A more effective way to get to know those who are agents of hospital discharge is to do some spade work. Visit hospitals. Learn who makes home healthcare referrals. Find out what process they use. Become known to these decision makers. Things like a free lunch or a cocktail party are good vehicles for getting to know these people beyond a name and a title. Be creative about establishing liaison between your business and the movers and shakers at the area hospitals. Remember: More deals are closed on a golf course than in a board room.

6.Dialogue

Aim for quality not quantity. While you want everyone in the medical profession to know you and the services you offer, it is better to get to know one or two physicians well than to spread yourself too thinly. If you try to reach out to too many sources at once, you may end up impressing none of the decision makers.

David Frey, author of *How to Make It Rain Referrals* warns his clients: "It's better to choose only one local family physician and become good friends with him than trying to be friends with ten physicians haphazardly." Cultivating a good working relationship takes time. Focus closely on just a few promising referral sources at first.

People like to talk about themselves, their families, and their hobbies. Learn about your referring agents and ask about these topics. Then really listen.

7. Social Media

While social media is a powerful marketing tool (more on that in a later chapter) nothing can replace the personal touch. Instead of counting on social media as a main marketing tool, use it as a device to inform decision makers about your services and offer a "virtual tour" of your facility for those who haven't the time or the inclination to take the actual tour.

8. Incentives

The famous sales person, Zig Ziggler advised: "You can get everything in life you want if you just help enough other people get what they want." What a valuable lesson this is in seeking referrals!

Referrals should be a mutually beneficial experience. If hospital agents who refer clients to your business get something in return they will remember you and be far more likely to refer your business again.

Focus on how you can help the individual or group that referred. It might be referrals to that physician's business. It could be media exposure. It might be a perk like a free lunch or some volunteer work. It could be a thank you gift. You are limited only by your imagination.

Incentives could include something as simple as passing out each other's business cards or brochures or occasionally referring clients. It could be something more deliberate, planned and organized like sharing booths at healthcare fairs, conventions, or events. You might offer advertising space on your blog or local media. Working together to create a joint referral plan benefits both businesses.

You might organize networking events or social evenings for your referring agents. Invite them to a free luncheon and guest speaker.

9. **Volunteer**

You have skills and facilities which may be of use to the hospital or physician who is the referring agent. One hand washes the other.

Volunteer the use of a piece of equipment or a staff member or set aside time to volunteer your services.

10. Provide a "Test Drive"

Car dealers and vacuum cleaner sales people learned this marketing technique ages ago. The best way to convince a potential referring individual or group of the worth of your service is to let them "test drive" it. The form may vary with the individual or group. Invite a potential client to enjoy the services of your business for a week-end or an overnight visit. Invite the referring individual and family to dine at your facility.

When they see how well things are working they will became raving fans.

11. Keeping Referral Sources Up to Date

Working with a referral source is an ongoing activity.

It is a relationship rather than an occasion or event. It requires dedication and persistence. It is vital to check back with your referral sources regularly. Keep them informed of any changes to your services, your staff and your physical plant. Make sure they have the most recent business cards and brochures. Take the time to discuss changes, additions and deletions and to address questions or concerns they may have.

Difficulties with Getting Referrals

1. Discovering who are the decision makers in the referral process is time-consuming and not always an easy task. Institutions like hospitals often make this a convoluted process on purpose.

2. Learning hospital priorities for home healthcare is important if you are to sell your service. If you have no idea what the hospital needs for a particular patient providing it becomes next to impossible. Meet with the potential client, the family, and the physician.

3. Making yourself known. If you are new to the area or to the business, getting yourself known is an ongoing and puzzling problem. A mentor or friend in the business is a real asset. If you have neither think about hosting an event.

4. Getting past the "gatekeeper". Almost every office has one. He/she may be official or self-acknowledged. It is definitely worth getting to know this person and acknowledging the gatekeeper's power.

5. Handling the referral process efficiently. In order to set up a referral process that works and does not waste time, it is critical that you understand the referral process and how it work and then function within the guidelines.

6. Not getting bogged down in issues. Remember: Their hospital; their rules. Learn to make the process work for you.

7. Discovering which technique works best: Have more than one technique at the ready and take the time to find out which marketing technique is going to work best.

8. Avoiding coming off sounding like a stereotypical "sales" person. This is the kiss of death. Remember: You are not selling something. You are providing a vital and needed service! Avoid being aggressive, manipulative, intrusive, or pushy. Be interested in the people with whom you are meeting. You are there to offer a service which their patients need.

9. Getting ongoing meetings with the physician. Physicians are busy people. So you must be clear why it is so crucial — not just for you but also for the physician — that you meet with him. Find out if the physician delegates home healthcare referrals to someone in the office and arrange to meet with that person. Remember: The physician holds the power to veto office staff decisions.

10. Speaking the same language: Let the referring agent know you share background, concerns, and empathy for the job they do. If they are speaking patient care and you are speaking

sales then the conversation is doomed.

Chapter Five: Using Social Media Effectively

Social media is changing the way we communicate and the way we are perceived, both positively and negatively. Every time you post a photo, or update your status, you are contributing to your own digital footprint and personal brand.
~Amy Jo Martin

What is Social Media?

Social media includes any and all websites and applications that allow users to create and share content and do social networking.

Why Bother?

- Over 60% of North American businesses — large and small — use at least one form of social media.

- Those who do not have a business website will be left behind by those who do.

- Twitter alone has 255 million active users. They send 500 million tweets every single day.

- There are more than 50 million Facebook Pages. India alone has a hundred million Facebook users. 72% of online adults visit Facebook at least twice a month.
- Google+ has 540 million actively users.
- 84% of women and 50% of men are active users of Pinterest.
- There are a billion YouTube users-80% of them are American. Six billion hours of YouTube are watched each month.
- 77% of Internet users read blogs. Nearly seven million people have blogs.
- Twenty billion photos have been uploaded to Instagram.
-

How Social Media Can Help

Social media is an amazing tool, but it's really the face-to-face interaction that makes a long-term impact.

~Felicia Day

1. **Social media provides another way for potential clients to learn about your business.**

Your website, your blog, Facebook… provide you with a way to get the word out about your home healthcare business. Social media has the potential to send all sorts of traffic to your website. There is no faster and less expensive way to become known in your community.

2. **Social media allows you to set up a dialogue with clients and potential clients.**

Lots of sites focus on a specific niche market. Chat rooms, blogs, networking and social news sites are dedicated to specific niches. You can speak directly to these people whom your business has the ability to serve.

3. **You become an expert in your field.**

The more you publish blogs, articles, guest articles on related websites, responses to specific concerns, information about new products and services specific to home healthcare business the more you become known as someone to turn to.

4. **Social media helps you and your business build client trust.**

As you become known as someone with knowledge and competence in your field, potential and present clients become increasingly trusting in what you have to say.

5. **Social media helps you and your business establish a more personal relationship with clients and potential clients.**

By using blogs, chats, advice, answering questions, suggesting resources, you prove to your niche market that your business is not just — or even mainly — about making money. Your chief goal is to provide a needed service to a specific clientele.

6. **Social media provides an avenue for instant recognition.**

Remember how young your kids were when they first recognized the Golden Arches logo? Social media provides small businesses like yours with an opportunity to air your brand. Your name, your logo, your business slogan will become instantly recognizable to potential clients. This kind of advertising is priceless.

7. Social media provides a level playing field for small businesses.

Thanks to social media, small businesses can compete with big companies. In the past, this was almost impossible. Small to medium sized companies just did not have the advertising and marketing budget to complete with larger companies. The potential is there for your website, YouTube, Facebook, Instagram, Pinterest or your blog to go viral. Your business could get an enormous amount of traffic.

8. Social media is an economical way to make your business known.

Social media marketing is incredibly inexpensive compared to other means of advertising.

9. Social media reaches a huge, global audience.

Social media reaches people all over the world. Whether you focus on a local or an international target market the cost is the same.

10. You can use social media marketing as a do-it-yourself project.

With a small investment in time and education, you can soon be setting up your own social media accounts and updating your text.

11. Social media marketing can be kept fresh and interesting.

With formal advertising, the cost is so high changes do not often occur. However, social media sites can be changed frequently. You can do it yourself with little expenditure of time or money. People will return often to see what is new and they will tell their friends.

12. **Social media allow for a personal touch.**
Whether it is interviews with clients or their families or a testimonial from a healthcare professional, social media sites let you have face-to-face time with clients and others.

13. **Social media allows you to explain yourself and your services**

Businesses often underuse social media because they are afraid of negative comments and critical feedback. However, social media offers a means of explaining, fixing a misinterpretation, righting a wrong and learning from a situation as a means of improving a situation.

When you reply, you are seen as person who cares. You become known as someone who wants to make a client happy. You are seen not just as a company spokesperson but also a real person with feelings. Social media provides the avenue for a dialogue or a conversation.

14. Social media allows you to show and tell.

With the potential for photos, brochures, a video, a podcast, a virtual tour, a slide show, chatting…social media allows you to show off the best and most interesting features of your business to audiences all over the world. Moreover, information can be quickly and easily updated so your presentation is always fresh and current.

How to Get Started

The worst step in getting started is no step at all.

If you tackle social media like you would a real life event you will experience greater success. You need to jump in and get started. If you went to a course, sat in a corner, and did not participate, what would you expect to learn? Not much. Right? But if you rolled up your sleeves, got involved and talked to others about what they were doing imagine how much more you'd learn and how much more confident you'd feel. If you set out convinced social media will work for your company, you won't be disappointed. Social media will work as effectively as you are prepared to make it work. You've got to become involved if you want results.

If you do it yourself the cost is small to none. You need to decide, however, what your time is worth. It might be worth your while to hire someone to help with social media marketing — at least at the outset.

1. Take stock:

Before you get started take stock of your goals. Your answers will affect how you get started and how you set up your social media site(s).

o What do you hope to get out of social media?

o Why are you doing this?

o Do you hope to generate increased business revenue?

o Will you use social media for customer service?

o Are you intending to build relationships with clients?

o Do you want to increase client confidence in your expertise?

o Will you be answering client questions and/or improving your client trust in your business expertise?

o Will you be writing content?

o How will you publish your writing?

2. Be interesting!

Tell your business story in a way that clients and potential clients can relate. How and why did you start your home healthcare business? What interesting things have occurred? What are your future plans?

3. Be consistent, current and generous.

Give your readers good, useful, up to date content. Give them more than they expect. Treat your readers like royalty.

4. Use content to generate responses.

Think of your social media content as a vehicle to help others and to create a reaction. Use social media as a springboard for getting to know your readers as people.

5. Baby steps. Rome was not built in a day.

Start with one website and gradually add other social media as you are able to handle the workload. Do one site well rather than several poorly.

6. Learn from others.

Find a trusted colleague, friend, or mentor and learn from him/her. We all started out knowing little about social media and grew from there.

7. Write for your known clients first.

When you are deciding who to write for choose your oldest, most loyal clients and write what they would enjoy hearing. If you build it they will come...other readers will follow and bring new questions for you to address.

8. Do what you would do at a fancy dinner party.

Read the social media of others in your field. Don't be afraid to ask to publish others' work. This generates links to their website.

9. Ask to be a guest writer for others' blogs.

This gets you and your website known and generates links for others' sites as well. The result is increased traffic all round. It's a win-win situation.

10. A picture is worth a thousand words.

Learn how to pin Pinterest and attach pictures and insert graphics and videos. It will increase traffic to your website.

11. Strike a friendly tone.

Be honest, helpful and friendly. Write as if you were talking to a friend. Write the way you'd like to be written to.

12. KISS

Keep vocabulary simple and sentences short. Write content appropriate for your audience. Don't make your audience work to try and figure out what you are saying.

13. Be indispensable.

Write content that is so useful your readers will want to save it and share it with others.

14. Share something small and useful every day.

Over time those little things grow into a huge volume of knowledge.

15. Be a lifelong learner.

Be on the lookout for seminars, speeches, conventions, conferences, and demonstrations that will teach you new things about social media.

16. It's not necessary to be original all the time.

There's value in sharing the current research and writing in your discipline. This shows you are knowledgeable and willing to showcase the writing of others.

17. Be patient.

Everything will not come together immediately. You won't start with a huge audience. But, it will grow.

18. Be daring.

You aren't going to break anything. Don't be afraid to try things.

19. Be yourself.

It's a good strategy to read the blogs and websites of others to learn about content, tone, and style but don't copy their content or style. Be yourself.

20. Choose the social media platform that works best for your business, your readers, and your topic.

There are many options. Survey them to get a feel for each and then choose the one that works best.

21. Don't overthink it.

Don't over complicate the task or your writing. Write for the sheer joy of helping your readers.

22. Evaluate the competition.

Take the time to look at the websites of your competitors.

- What works for them?
- What topics do they address?
- What is aesthetically appealing about their sites?
- What style do they use?
- What is the one thing you'd most like to have in your website?

Tools and Tips for Social Media Marketing of Your Home Healthcare Business

1. Easy Media Gallery Pro

A picture is worth a thousand words. Use photos and sales promotion materials to enhance your text and strengthen your message. Easy Media Gallery Pro is an user friendly WordPress plugin. This tool lets you upload images into galleries for posting online in one step. Easy Media Gallery Pro offers several configurations, editing options and a wide range of display functionality. You can simply embed into any blog post or other social media site.

2. Hang w/

Do you want an easy way to live stream or create a video for your website?

Hang w/ is an app for your iPhone or Android. It allows you to live stream at the push of a button. Then you can post it directly to your Facebook page. You can send it to others who have the Hang w/ app or you can post it on YouTube.

3. Flipagram

With this tool you can create short video stories. Flipagram lets you use your photos and add background music. These fifteen-second videos can be posted on Twitter, Instagram and YouTube.

The Flipagram app works on both Android and iPhone. Download the easy-to-use app. Select the photos from your phone or Facebook and create your video.

4. Swayy

If you are trying to find interesting and useful content to shares on your website Swayy can help.

Log in with your Twitter ID, or Facebook account. Swayy analyzes your audience and shows the most popular trending topics of your audience.

5. Social Media Dashboard

Time management is a major problem with social media. Social media dashboards like: HootSuite, TweetDeck or Social Oomph, help you manage your social media time. Social media dashboard tools let you to set up alerts and notifications. You can create groups, skim text fast, and schedule updates. You can automate some processes making business contact smooth and efficient.

Things to Avoid when Using Social Media for your Home Healthcare Business

1. Don't Forget a Plan

Unfortunately, in their ignorance and naiveté, many small business owners leap into social media without doing any research. They've been told it was a must and they are eager to get started. So they skip the planning phase. As with all marketing tools, it's important to familiarize yourself with the network(s) you are joining and develop a plan of action to achieve your marketing goals.

2. Don't Exaggerate or Distort the Truth

It is easy to get caught up in one-upmanship on the social media. You want your business to be popular. So you stretch the truth a little. Embellishing things may get you more traffic. This is never a good idea. It is likely to hurt your reputation and make your brand less credible.

3. Don't Be Self-Centred

Social media failure results from your making your site all about YOU and your home healthcare business. Instead, focus on what you can do to help your clients and potential clients. Your social media presence is about for your brand, not you personally. Let your visitors see a little personality in your interactions. But don't focus your attention on you. Think about what your readers would profit from knowing. Offer your expertise to help others while sharing a little of your personal side.

4. Don't Spam

Social media spamming to avoid include: unsolicited sales pitches, repeated posting the same updates, and sending private messages after you've been requested not to.

5. Don't Be Slangy, Suggestive, Obnoxious or Profane

Business social media sites that attack the competition are unpopular. So, too, are ones that use slangy lingo, profanity, and are obnoxious or offensive. Social media for business should be professional.

6. Don't be Guilty of TMI

You know how you feel when a casual acquaintance or neighbor tells you confidential information you don't know them well enough for them to be sharing such intimate details of their lives. Well, social media is a lot like that. When you're using social media for business, sharing bits of your personality is an effective way to build rapport. But, there is a definite line between sharing some facts and divulging personal information. Treat what you're posting as a personal message to a cherished client or a mentor. If you wouldn't tell this client in a conversation the information has no place on your social media site. Too much information makes receivers feel uncomfortable. It is unprofessional — and creepy!

7. Don't Treat Social Media as Advertising

Social media networks are very different from other business marketing tools. Share information about your business experiences, your business products and services. But do it from the point of view of helping others — not a hard sell of your home healthcare business. Your goals are to help others and to encourage your social media friends and followers to pass your promotions on to their network of friends and followers.

8. Practice Social Media Best Practices

There are no rigid rules about what you should and shouldn't do on social media. Best practices will nurture growing, engaged followers:

a) Make effective use data and analytics. They are there for you to use. Try to get as much insight as possible from not only your visitors and from your competition. Note things like users who mention your company, who is regularly posting about your business, who has a lot of followers, and who purchased your home healthcare services, what follow up you might do to help them, how visitors who did not purchase your service might benefit from information you could share, what loyalty incentives you could offer to long-time clients...

b) Aim to reach your loyal followers. Don't worry about the other millions out there on the social media. Seek a smaller number of loyal followers. Consider your social media relationships like you would real-life relationships. Bonds are not made overnight. They take time and trust to solidify. It is most effective to invest consistently small amounts of time over a longer period on social media rather than creating one huge project.

c) Nurture local contacts. Use social media to reach potential clients in your geographic area by using content specifically targeting your community. This is a way for you to relate directly to the potential clients who will be in a position to use your home healthcare services.

d) Plan ahead. Create a calendar of what you will be sharing for the next month. That way you won't be scrambling to figure out what to post every day. Figure in holidays: Thanksgiving, Christmas, Valentine's Day, Easter as well as local community promotion days. If there is a "Seniors' Day" or a "Family Health Day" or "Grandparents' Day" or a "Health Expo Week" what great times to promote your home healthcare business.

e) Don't reinvent the wheel. Make use of what you already have. Take content you've already created or content that clients, service providers or even the competition or related businesses have produced. This makes less work for you and celebrates the efforts of others!

f) Engage your visitors. Post quizzes, polls, or contests. Try running a live Q&A or a trivia competition. Be creative with the kind of content and outreach you provide!

g) When you have established connections with followers, begin offers to turn social media activities into service offers. Personalize offers to specific individuals or groups. AARP members, those who belong to the local seniors' center, or gym or library are good target groups for your services. Ask yourself: Where in this community would my target market hang out?

h) React quickly. As soon as you receive feedback on social media, act quickly. Respond to compliments, queries and complaints. Honor the fact that they have taken the time to communicate. Address concerns and maintain or repair the credibility of your home healthcare business. By responding quickly, you establish and maintain an image of a home healthcare business owner who sincerely cares about client and potential client. You prove you will respond honestly to feedback and criticism and that you can and will make changes.

i) Personalize offers and tweets to individual customers. Make sure your home healthcare business has a unique character. Above all: Be authentic. You are your home healthcare business' greatest asset. Potential clients want relationships with people—not with a brand. Be the personal voice of your home healthcare business online. Nurture trust. Aim at readers of your social media liking you.

Chapter Six: Giving Clients and Employees the Red-Carpet Treatment

It's amazing how few people ever hear those three little,
important words: I appreciate you!
~Levo La Gue

Remember watching the Academy Awards? The stars arrive in sleek shiny limos. The door to the limo is opened and out steps a Hollywood celebrity — onto a bright red carpet. Imagine how special that person feels. Everyone's eyes are glued to the beautiful people special enough to warrant the red carpet.

When the Queen or other visiting royalty tour a foreign country, they are given the red carpet treatment. "Red-carpet treatment" has become synonymous with special treatment given to those who are deemed worthy of that recognition.

A red carpet is most often associated with the path taken by <u>heads of state</u> on ceremonial and formal occasions. More recently the red carpet has been extended to use by VIPs and celebrities at formal events.

Red-carpet treatment has its roots in history. Showman Sid Grauman may have created the Hollywood's red-carpet tradition, by placing out a red walkway in front of his Egyptian Theatre for the 1922 premiere of *Robin Hood* starring Douglas Fairbanks

The idea of a red carpet goes back to 458 B.C. In the play *Agamemnon*, written by Aeschylus a Trojan War hero who returns home to find a crimson carpet rolled out for him by his wife. He is reluctant to walk on it as he sees it as the gods' walkway.

Think about how special your clients, your employees, your service providers would feel if you aimed at giving them the red-carpet treatment every day!

Studies have shown that employees value recognition above even money and perks. They want to feel acknowledged and appreciated for their efforts. When you do that a strange thing happens: They try harder to please and they begin to treat clients, colleagues — and even their employer with more respect.

Make each day about ensuring that your clients, employees, colleagues and service providers have an extraordinary experience.

Whether you are a CEO, a mid-level manager, or a team leader strive to get your home healthcare business to deliver consistently excellent client service.

In her soon-to-be-released book, *501 Ways to Roll out the Red Carpet for Your Customers* author Donna Cutting discusses ways to WOW your patients, your employees, your guests and your service providers.

Providing an outstanding experience for your clients is critical to the survival of your home healthcare business. The truth is: Today's potential clients have more choices than ever. And, thanks to social media, they also have an important and influential voice in their every comment — and criticism. Their posted comments, queries, and criticisms are read by thousands who have the potential to become future clients — or not!

Red-carpet customer service means being treated like a super star or a beloved relative. When you roll out the red carpet for your clients, you're treating them as if they're important, special, and like treasured friends or much-revered members of your family. Your aim is to do this consistently. You want your clients' undying loyalty. So you set out to earn rave reviews, referrals, and continuing service.

A 2011 study by Harris Interactive shows almost 90% of clients changed to a different service provider because of ONE bad experience with that business. In 2007 only a little over half of the clients would have taken such action. What is happening? Customer service has deteriorating OR clients are becoming empowered with additional choices and the resolve not to sit back and accept mediocre treatment.

With today's social media sadly poor client service reports are read by twice as many people as is praise for excellent client experience, according to a study done by White House Office of Consumer Affairs. The good news is that if you WOW your clients with red-carpet treatment over half of them will willingly recommend your home healthcare business to others — regardless of whether you charge more for you service than your competitors, as shown by the research of Harris Interactive/Right Now 2010 "Customer Experience Impact Report".

Research shows that businesses spend inordinate amounts of time, money, and people resources on marketing and sales. Imagine what would happen if you spent just a fraction of that marketing money on ensuring your clients are happy with your service and eager to give referrals!

A *real sale* is made *after* you earn your client's business. As Don Draper on "Mad Men" says, "The day you sign a client is the day you start losing one." Constant vigilance is the price of survival and prospering in the home healthcare business. We all acknowledge the truth of this statement. The problem is: Who has the time?

Just about everyone today has a long to-do list. Adding to it creative ways to roll out the red carpet for clients is not always seen as the priority it should be.

The best employee and client experiences start at the top with owners, CEO's, and managers. Even if you see a definite need to give your employees and clients continuous red-carpet treatment, you have to deal with the realities of champagne dreams and a beer budget.

How can you be expected to design an extraordinary client experience when you have too many other pressing things to do? How can you be expected to create exemplary employee experiences with too few resources? How can you be expected to implement a red-carpet experience that honors your service providers when you have when you're on information and technological overload? If every slot of your day already scheduled, how can you make red-carpet treatment of all stakeholders in your business a reality?

Here is the first piece of good news: You don't have to re-invent the wheel.

Find out about those people who have visualized and implemented fantastic ideas to surprise and delight their clients.

Be warned though: Revolutionizing the entire customer experience takes planning and commitment, a strong vision and a supportive team. You have to hire the right people. Get them involved by engaging, empowering, and encouraging them. Some will see this as rewarding. Some will view it as fun. Others will, unfortunately, view it as unprofessional, beneath them, or worse, fawning and pandering! Hire those who see this as worthwhile and are committed to providing red-carpet treatment. Then make sure they too receive red-carpet treatment that lets them know their efforts are acknowledged and valued.

As the owner of a home healthcare business you have an awesome job. Singlehandedly you can shape the culture of your business.

You can engineer it so everyone who comes into contact with your business—clients, visitors, employees, service providers, potential clients, medical personnel—all receive the red-carpet treatment. Small actions can make a big impact! But, it takes someone like you to get the ball rolling—or the red carpet rolled out!

Remember the story about the cabbie who was slowly, one compliment, one cheery comment at a time bringing love back to New York City? He knew small gestures can have a big impact.

In Donna Cutting's newest book, *501 Ways to Roll out the Red Carpet for Your Customers* examples of how to use hiring strategies, employee engagement techniques, and other client loyalty ideas for laying providing everyone who is a stakeholder in your home healthcare business with the red-carpet experience.

I know what you're thinking. Your budget is tight. How are you ever going to find the money for this red-carpet treatment? Well, here's the good news! It doesn't have to cost a million dollars to provide your clients and employees with a million-dollar impact.

Remember: The way to innovate inside your home healthcare business is to look at other businesses — even those not connected in any way to healthcare — for inspiration. Borrow ideas from outside the healthcare field to the surprise and delight of *your* clients, employees, service providers and the community you serve. When you come upon an idea that worked well, write it down. Then be sure to celebrate your results! Next, try a new idea.

You will find heartening results when you look. There are red-carpet stories of people in businesses just like yours that are creating daily extraordinary experiences for their clients, employees and other stakeholders.

A good example of an inexpensive but effective red-carpet idea is shared in *The Celebrity Experience: Insider Secrets to Delivering Red-Carpet Customer Service.* This is shared by a market management team in the field of education. High Point University greets expected visitors by rolling out the red carpet symbolically. When visitors pull into the parking lot at High Point, the first thing they see is a personal welcome sign. The potential student, parent, or special guest is directed to park in a space bearing a personalized welcome sign. Visitors feel so special and WOW-ed by this experience that they often pose beside the sign!

Welcome sign at a parking space, at a reception desk, or on your business' marque are surely giving visitors the red-carpet treatment at little to no cost.

That's just one of many ideas out there that might work well in your home healthcare business.

Everyone loves to receive attention and recognition.
Birthdays can be big events in your business.
Celebrate all birthdays with cake, a small gift, a song,
a card signed by everyone in your business. This is
red-carpet treatment. Selecting a bunch of small
ideas — one idea at a time — and gradually
implementing them is what red-carpet treatment is all
about.

Where to find these? Borrow ideas. Check others'
websites. Talk to people whose business culture you
admire. Read resource books like the ones I have
listed. Be always on the alert for something you
experienced that WOW-ed you. Then ask yourself:
Would this be red-carpet treatment that would work
in my home healthcare business? How can I tweak
this idea?

First impressions — like the personalized sign — are
important. These might include:

- A personalized welcome package
- A message from the owner left on your
  phone, or in your work area

- A visit from the company owner or CEO just to see that things a fine
- A welcome-to-the building "cocktail" meet-and-greet
- A formal staff-led tour of the facility
- A special lunch on your first day there
- Your very own ID badge or bracelet

Building a foundation of excelling, going beyond mere basic service, and personalized service are things that red-carpet businesses make a priority. Here's an example from a cleaning business that provides red-carpet treatment:

> *We once received a call from a customer in Mount Alto, W.Va. who had called two other companies but never talked to a live person and never received a call back. The customer was pleased to talk to a live person and the fact The Red Carpet Treatment worked around their schedule, making an evening appointment when the client returned from work, was much appreciated.*

That personal touch doesn't cost so much. In fact, hiring a person or service to field calls might well be cheaper than one of those irritating automated systems that de-personalize your business.

Another owner commented on his business' red-carpet treatment:

Customers do receive the personal touch when they hire us. They deal directly, one-on-one with me, The Owner, or someone connected to my family-run business. Whoever talks to them about their questions or concerns is more than just an employee. Our company owners and employees take pride in what we do. With 23 years' experience, we know what we are doing and we are committed to ensuring that, from start to finish, you get red-carpet treatment.

Another way to provide red-carpet treatment is to turn everyday events into special occasions. We've already mentioned birthdays and "first day" at your home healthcare moments. What about a client who is returning from hospital? An employee who just had a baby? Landmark anniversaries as a client or an employee? Mother's Day? Father's Day? Grandparents' Day? Red Hat Day? Honor Veterans' Day... Constantly seek ways to turn mundane moments into memorable ones.

Put an extra flourish on an everyday service. For example a barber offers a free shave with each haircut. A hair stylist serves wine or non-alcoholic drinks while your hair is being colored or permed or styled. A restaurant offers its loyal clients the eleventh meal on them! This is a 10% discount but how much more exciting is this stamped card turned in for a free meal?

Grocery stores that offer free coffee while you shop or to go make customers feel special. Organizations , businesses and church that offer free babysitting and child activities make parents feel special.

Aim to offer flawless service. However, there will be things that go wrong. Meet these with grace, style, and empathy. Listen to the client. Acknowledge that something went wrong. Apologize. Promise to make it right. Tell how you are going to do this and do it.

Your home healthcare business will flourish if you never miss a chance to give standing ovations to your staff, your service providers and your clients. The more you offer authentic and warranted praise, the more your business reputation will go up and the more referrals you will receive. Work at providing red-carpet treatment that will turn prospects into customers and customers into raving fans.

Chapter Seven: Giving Staff the Star Treatment

I've learned that people will forget what you said.

They will forget what you did.

But people will never forget how you made them

feel

~Maya Angelo

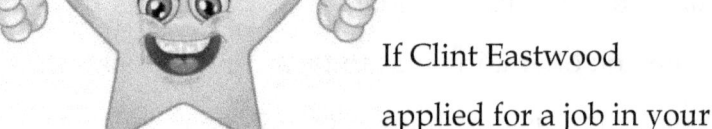 If Clint Eastwood applied for a job in your home healthcare business, how would you react? If you're like most people, you'd drop whatever you were doing and approach him, smiling, ready and eager to have him on your team. If Doris Day walked into your book store, you'd eagerly

give her the grand tour and explain all the perks of working in your book store. If Tom Hanks called to ask for information about a job posting your answers immediate, cheerful, and enthusiastic. Right?

This is exactly what I am talking about. Every employee — prospective, just hired, and long-time — should be treated like a star.

Employees who are treated like stars will be loyal to a company that may not pay as well as the competition but makes sure its employees are well treated by management and by the clients. Even more important than money is a workplace where employees look forward to coming to work.

How can you make sure this is the case? In his book, *The 9 Elements of Highly Effective Employee Praise*, author Jeff Haden suggests several practical, common sense strategies including:

Ditch Employee of the Month

Lose the Employee-of-the-Month program. His rationale? No one cares about it! Everybody thinks it is lame and phony. Instead he states that businesses like yours give genuine, earned recognition. Formal recognition programs never deliver what they promise. Employees see them insincere. It's like a company had to implement a recognition program. So that's what they came up with.

Give Real Praise

Haden writes: "Generic praise is nice but specific praise is wonderful." This means: Don't just tell an employee he/she did a good job. Tell the employee <u>how</u> the job was great. That way the employee knows you pay attention to what is being done—and what to do next time.

Bosses who give "scheduled" warm fuzzies are seen as insincere. It's like: Oh! It's one o'clock. I have to pass through the facility and murmur non-specific warm comments. Haden advises: "Never praise for the sake of praising. It's obvious to everyone, and you lessen the impact when you really do mean what you say."

Go Hunting

Dealing with employees is not all that different from dealing with kids. Manage by wandering around. Catch them being good. Praise immediately and publicly. Put it in writing in the employee file.

Be Surprising

Expected presents are nice. Unexpected ones are even more special. Praise or presents — if they are unexpected they are huge! Receiving a surprise card, letter, or visit from the owner to compliment an employee on special service is a major occurrence.

Spread the Goodwill

Find ways to spread good news about outstanding employee performance. But, also be aware that some employees don't immediately stand out. Make a special effort to "catch them being good". This kind of encouragement may well be the turning point for a poor performer.

Create a Culture of Recognition

Make recognition a priority. Nurture employee success and acknowledgement of it. For example: Share two examples of employees' action that should be recognized and praised each day. Get other employees and clients involved in "recognize an angel" moments.

Snowball Effect

When praise and recognition are freely and honestly given it produces two reactions. Recognized employees work harder to receive even more recognition. Those who see peers recognized have a natural competitiveness to accomplish things worthy of praise.

Those who "caught others being good" work even harder to see others' good deeds and report them as they too get recognition.

A special bond develops between reporters and reported.

The entire business culture improves! Win win win!

Don't Bulk Order Employee Recognition

Every employee accepts praise differently. Some like public praise. Others prefer written acknowledgement. Get to know your employees so you can tailor your acknowledgement to the comfort level of that specific employee. It is not a "one size fits all" process. Choose the recognition that has the greatest impact for each individual employee.

Nothing Succeeds Like Success

Recognizing effort and achievement is self-fulfilling. When you do an outstanding job of recognizing your employees, they perform better — and so do you.

Look at Your Business as an Employee for a Day

View your home healthcare business through the eyes of an employee. See what your employees experience on a daily basis. Ask a friend to pose as a client and report her/his experiences with your employee. Do this frequently varying employees. See how your employee treats new customers that makes your clients feel like stars. See what challenges employees are faced with.

Surveys of employees in the 1980's and again in the early 2000's showed their number one priority — ahead of money, promotions and benefits — was to feel appreciated, acknowledged and recognized for their efforts.

Employers consistently expected that employees were looking for tangible rewards. They were always wrong. What employees needed to feel like stars was "soft" things: A word of appreciation, a surprise card or letter, public acknowledgement of a job well done. They wanted to know their bosses took the time to get to know them as people first and employees second.

How to Treat Employees and Clients Like STARS

 In her book, *The Celebrity Experience: Insider Secrets to Delivering Red Carpet Customer Service*, author and marketing expert, Donna Cutting, makes these suggestions for giving your clients and employees the star treatment:

Give Them a Red Carpet Arrival.

When a celebrity arrives on the red carpet for the Oscar, a movie premiere or a charity event, the crowd treats it like a big deal! Fans and paparazzi by the throngs line up waving, calling out greetings, and in general making that person feel special, welcomed, valued. Why do we not do that for employees and new clients? We can line up to greet them, form a receiving line, take their picture and post it for everyone to see. Them and get to know they are now part of your home healthcare business.

Sadly, when most of us arrive at a place of business, we're lucky if we can even get someone to acknowledge us. If instead, we treated clients and employees and service providers like stars by showing them you're glad they came we'd have them at "hello" for sure.

How do we do this? It needn't be a big deal. It can be as simple as smiling, walking out toward them and greeting them. Most people don't need a red carpet or paparazzi, A smile, eye contact, a handshake, and a friendly greeting is enough!

Call Them By Name.

Motivational speaker, marketing guru, and author, Dale Carnegie, discusses the power of knowing and using someone's name. It makes them feel important. Remembering employees' and clients' names and using them each time you talk to them is huge. Remember the bar on "Cheers"? It was known as the place "where everyone knows my name" and "treats me like family". That's the kind of STAR treatment your colleagues, employees and clients want.

If you make names a top priority, and you'll find remembering them easier than you think. Devise unique ways of using someone's name.

Remember the welcome signs at High Point University? The facility welcomes all its expected guests with their own parking space bearing their name. Photos in the lobby, a personalized ID badge, a welcome package with the person's name on the front and a personalized welcome letter inside is a big deal for new people.

Using a person's name can work in other areas such as a special dish named after that person. How about some of your products after your best customers? Now that's the star treatment!

Think about how special you felt checking in to a hotel or a conference or a new business or a new store and you were called by name. This is the way to make clients and employees feel like stars.

Remember and Refer

If, in addition to an employee, client, or service provider's name, you also recall details about their hobbies, children, wife, favorite food…it makes them feel like stars.

A grocery store manager remembered one of his grump senior citizens had been to Denver to visit her daughter. So, he asked her about the trip. The transformation was immediate and unbelievable. She smiled. She talked. She showed him pictures! From that moment on they called one another by name and always went out of their way to ask about each other's families.

Little pieces of information can make a huge difference. Ordinary people feel special. Just pay attention and recall the information. Some employers even keep a file and update it with new events in an employee's life.

I always feel like a star when the receptionist at my doctor's office calls me by name and asks about my kids or the maître d' at a favourite restaurant calls me by name, seats me at the table I like and says that my favourite waiter will be right over with my favourite wine. I feel like a star when the singer at a favourite club calls me by name — and plays a song I particularly like.

Cater to Their Personal Preferences.
When one star travels he is impressed that hotels, entertainment facilities stock his favorite beverage. Another is pleased to find black jelly beans provided. While your employees and clients may not be as picky as the star who insists on all the brown M&M's being removed from his candy dish, everyone has specific likes and dislikes. Surprise and delight your employees and clients by remembering the little things. This lets them know you are paying attention and you care enough to bother.

Author and keynote speaker, Dave Timmons, earned the banking business of a potential client after giving him two baseballs signed by the members of his grandsons' favorite sports team.

One hotel dining room supervisor overheard a guest say she liked blood oranges. He secretly sent some up to her room. She was, of course, surprised and delighted. When you give people the star treatment in this way, you and your business become unforgettable.

Gift Them!

At special events, stars get gift bags filled with products worth thousands. Businesses line up to be part of that gifting. The publicity is HUGE when super stars wear or use their product. This creates buzz.

While your clients and employees may not create the buzz super stars do gift bags for new hires and clients still make them feel special. They share their surprise and delight with friends and family. Given social media, they may share with thousands.

How do you get these products and services? Ask. Explain the potential publicity. Trade your free service—like a massage or a manicure—for another business' goods or services.

Look at the free press Ben & Jerry's gets when they hold a "Free Cone Day."

Think about it: What can you give your clients and employees that will get them talking about you—and the businesses that provided free services, free goods, or discount coupons?

Go one Step Beyond!

Make a commitment to your clients and employees to provide the best service, benefits, treatment. Then go beyond what you promised. Constantly be on the lookout for little ways to make your clients, employees and service providers feel like the most important person in the world.

This kind of star treatment creates loyal clients and employees. It also makes them raving fans of your home healthcare business. They will go out and spread the word about the incredible star treatment they receive!

It doesn't have to cost a lot to make those with whom your business deals feel like stars. What it takes is commitment and energy for you to make this happen. Their smiles of surprise and delight will make the effort worthwhile. Everyone likes to feel like a star!

Chapter Eight: Have Your Clients at Hello...and Good-bye

Remember the scene that spawned "You had me at hello!"? Tom Cruise as Jerry Maguire said:

But it wasn't complete, wasn't nearly close to being in the same vicinity as complete, because I couldn't share it with you. I couldn't hear your voice or laugh about it with you. I miss my -- I miss my wife.

We live in a cynical world, a cynical world, and we work in a business of tough competitors.

I love you. You -- complete me.

And I just had --

To which Dorothy said, "Shut up. Just shut up. You had me at hello."

First impressions or hellos are crucial. You never get a second chance to make a first impression. Research shows that people form their first impression of you within seven seconds. A 2014 study by the University of Glasgow says that it takes a half-second for people to make up their minds about you. You literally can have them...or not...at "Hello".

As owners of home healthcare businesses — or any business — you want to have every client at hello. You want them to feel eager to have your services, thankful to be allowed to stay in your own home because you are there and pleased and comfortable with the services you provide.

In fact, many businesses work very hard at entries: schools, hotels, entertainment facilities, sports centers, gymnasiums, social clubs...They do a terrific job of welcoming new members, guests, new clients. Unfortunately, these same businesses often do a bad job of guest departure or de-missions.

We've all had experiences where we were in long line ups to check out of a hotel because they were short-staffed or no one had thought to pre-deliver our bill for speedy checkout. We've stood in slow lines to collect luggage or hail a cab upon deplaning. We've stood in long lines at the supermarket while heaping carts ahead of us were laboriously checked through by one or two clerks while checkout stands remained closed.

Examples of Good Hellos

When it comes to hospitality, the food and beverage business sinks or swims on its ability to provide good hellos. The food and beverage trade is also part of other businesses like seniors' accommodation, hotels, inns, B & B's, campgrounds, entertainment, bowling alleys, movie theaters, schools, and fine arts centers. Food and beverage services can greatly enhance the quality and customer service of other businesses.

Businesses involved in travel know that travelers value thoughtful treatment and simple amenities. When they feel that they have received star treatment they will readily tell others. In this day of social media this sharing can be huge!

A local amateur theatre in a small North Carolina town really knows how to do great hellos. If you are a first time theatre attender at their facility, when you book your tickets you receive a personalized thank you letter from the president of the theatre council. This is followed by helpful information about parking, arrival time and the play you will be seeing. Prior to the event, depending on how far ahead you booked your seats, you'll receive several updates.

The theatre will provide information about good places to eat. They will even tell you what time you should leave your house based on expected traffic for that day. You may even preorder your drink for intermission. This all arrives in your inbox along with a map of the theatre so you can see where your seats are.

Many businesses could learn a lot about good hellos from this volunteer-organized facility!

Inconsistencies

Gone are the days when customers were satisfied with a smile, "please", "sir" and "thank you". Clients want star treatment. They expect memorable experiences and smooth, dynamic service. They expect routines will be efficient and standard practices will be faultless. They expect things will be customized to suit their needs and their requests. They want to feel like their business is appreciated. Businesses need to anticipate client needs and serve them accordingly.

Clients return and tell others about your business when you deliver what you promised when you promised it—and go above and beyond what clients expected.

They want the same consistent exemplary service every time. This is the sign of a good hello.

Clients get frustrated when their "first hello" is excellent but then the service is inconsistent.

Don't promise what you cannot deliver. It is important to provide consistently stellar service. Make it a point to be on the fast track for keeping up with trends that your customers may follow such as building personal assistance services for traveling customers or making special concessions for avid repeat consumers. Be sure you have items on hand so when your customer needs you and your products, everything's available. A customer who has to continuously wait for you to do your part may grow tired, no matter how loyal, and venture off to your competition. Keep customers loyal by focusing on them at all times.

Give your customers an outlet for telling you about poor experiences.

When you have customers who have had a negative experience, make it easy and clear for them to not only tell you about it but get it off their chest to you and not someone else. Don't patronize customers when they are disgruntled by shooing them off with little to no plans for recourse. Make it a point to correct issues that went wrong and look into those that could stand some improvement. Capture communication methods for keeping in contact with your customers so that you can alert them when changes and improvements occur.

Good Good-byes

While hellos are crucial to a business, last impression or good-byes may be what sticks with your clients or employees the most. *Recency Effect* is a psychological term. It states that, when asked to recall specific items on a list, people are more likely to first remember those that came at the end of the list.

You can make a smashing first impression and blow it all up with a poor last impression. Businesses often discount the importance of good-bye because they see it as final. Why worry? Too late now.

Hellos seem easier for businesses than good-byes. In truth, most home healthcare businesses pay no attention whatsoever to good-byes. What do they matter? Well they do!

With a good good-bye, clients, family, friends, community members, and service providers remember what a classy organization you run. Whether your client has died, gone to a more intensive service out of necessity, is moving to a different geographic location you do not serve or has improved enough not to need your services, or is actually dissatisfied with the service you provided, the way you bid them farewell speaks volumes.

Remember: You are all about helping your clients and providing what they need. When you say good-bye do it the way you'd bid farewell to a beloved relative. Clients, their families, friends and community members will long remember you took the time to wish them well, offer referral and transition services and let them know you would be available should they need you again.

Some businesses have the attitude, "Don't let the door hit you on your way out!" These are not facilities or services to which customers readily return. Clients expect good hellos and good-byes. They could well take a page from the "hello good-bye" book of a small theater company.

The team at the Durham Performing Arts Center in Durham, NC has its customers right from the first hello to the final good-bye.

Here's how they do it: When you arrive for a performance you'll be greeted by a group of smiling, friendly people in red-coats and top hats. Their entire purpose is to ensure that your every need is met while you're at the theater.

When you leave after the performance the red-coated group is outside the theater doors ready to send you off with a smile. They offer to hail cabs or get you to your car. They invite you back and ask about your theater experience to ensure you enjoyed yourself. If anything wasn't quite right, they note this and you will receive a follow up call to discuss what they can do to improve the situation. It's this kind of red-carpet treatment that brings people back to this facility and prompts them to tell their friends about their excellent evening out. This is a lesson in good hellos and good-bye small, mid-size and large businesses could learn from.

Why Are Good Good-byes Important?

Don't assume "good-bye" is forever. In fact, treat it as "See you soon!" Create business relationships where both client and employee feel like part of a business family. Consider relationships — current clients and past clients — top priority. Staying in touch with employee, client, and service provider contacts can be even more important after the relationship has ended. Managing business relationships is one of the best ways to make sure your business stays healthy. Many times, clients have moved their business elsewhere or employees have changed companies. If the good-bye was a good one, many have eventually returned to your business or they have referred clients to you.

Always leave the door open for their return. Don't speak poorly of them. Let them know you'd welcome them back. That is the sign of a good good-bye.

Treat a good-bye as a way to cement future business or to pave the way for a return of this client or employee. When you view good-byes this way, they are opportunities to promote your business and provide goodwill. They are not ends but transitions. If you do them with finesse they will net dividends for your home healthcare business.

People like to Associate with Businesses and People They Like

Take the time to relate to your client or employee. Treat him like a friend. Be genuine and interested. See him as a person first and part of your home healthcare business second. Making the effort is worth the time and energy. Ask questions and remember things that are important to clients and employees. Connect with them on a deeper level. People like to associate with those they like. They will find good-bye much harder if they genuinely like you.

A friend insisted on using the same realtor regardless of opportunities to purchase directly from an owner or deal with another realtor who had listed a place she found attractive. Why? She liked this realtor. She trusted her advice. They went to the same church. They used the same dog groomer. This realtor was excellent at hello and at sustaining a relationship. She made her clients feel like stars.

Spend Time Managing Contacts

Just as it is important to make clients and employees feel like stars, it is also important to spend time managing contacts. If your first experience with these contacts did not pan out, never assume this was "good-bye". Check back. Things change. Have a system. Managing present contacts will garner you new contacts. Nurtured contacts, clients, and employees can be great referrals in the future.

Careful Hires Nurture Good Hellos and Good-byes

How many employees merely follow the rules, do their job but never relate to your customers? My guess is plenty. Businesses spend billions of dollars encouraging clients to purchase goods and services. They spend little on keeping those clients happy, making them feel like stars and letting them know they are cherished and cared about.

When you are hiring people choose ones who will see clients as people first. Pick people who can communicate. Choose employees who empathize and are committed to making your clients and their colleagues feel like stars!

Look at Your Business as a Client

View your home healthcare business through the eyes of a client. See what your clients and customers experience on a daily basis from you and your employees.

Or ask a friend to pose as a client. Do this frequently. You have a customer at hello. It doesn't take much to have them at goodbye if you maintain steady, consistent, caring service that makes your clients feel like stars.

There is no Such Thing as Too Much Recognition

Whether it is hello, good-bye or something in between, keep in mind that there is no such thing as too much recognition. Clients, employees, service providers, volunteers, the lady next door who bakes you cookies all thrive on recognition for the things they do. Recognition might be verbal. It might be public or private — or both. It might be a handwritten note or a small gift or dinner.

When you treat people like stars they will remember that they were acknowledged and they will view you and your home healthcare business as a helpful, trusted friend and neighbor.

Chapter Nine: Making "Movie Moments" for Your Clients

We all have those movie moments that took us by surprise and delighted us. That's what making movie moments is all about. "Movie moments" make us want to run out and tell our friends to go and see that movie.

Remember *Grease*, *Jerry McGuire*, *Rocky*, or *The Empire Strikes Back*? These are moments that you'll never forget. You've probably talked about them with your friends. That's one of the reasons why those movies were so successful.

Just imagine if you could make those kinds of moments for your customers! "Movie moments" are ones that take your clients completely by surprise. These are the occasions that make clients see you and your homecare business in a new light.

Movie moments ignite an emotional response. Movie moments cause clients to tell their friends about what your company is doing!

If your home healthcare business can create "movie moments" for its clients, staff, and other stakeholders they will run right out and tell their friends and you will get referrals like you can't create with even the richest marketing budget.

What makes a "movie moment"? It's a positive, delightful, unexpected event. Here's an example: Rick Salmeron CEO of Salmeron Financial Services noticed how hot it was one day. It was so humid even air conditioners couldn't keep up. So, he had an idea. He delivered ice cream to his staff and customers. Guess what? People were surprised and delighted.

The event was such a hit that Rick Salermon now has scoops of ice-cream special delivered to clients all across USA during what he refers to as "National Ice Cream Week". From this one "movie moment" and entire "movie event" has spawned.

Thanks to social media, the nation-wide event is captured and posted on Facebook. Salermon calls it his Ice Cream Online Party. You can't buy this kind of positive publicity for your business!

Other Examples of "Movie Moments"

A keynote speaker at a women's club laughingly referred to the greeters as giving her the red carpet treatment. Imagine her surprise and delight the next time she returned to see a red carpet and the local press there to capture the event.

Having returned from helping a colleague at the opening to his healthcare facility, a friend was amused and surprised to receive his own mini carpet. This one was blue and a replica of the blue welcome mat at the entrance to his friend's healthcare store.

When a young couple stopped late one night at an Atlanta restaurant the manager told them he was sorry but the kitchen was closed for the evening.

As they turned to go the maître d' had an inspiration. He called them back and offered them a seat. The wait staff was requested to bring leftover appetizers and entrees from the kitchen. Staff continued to close up and the young couple enjoyed a veritable buffet. That maître d' transformed to potential lost customers into a "movie moment". The young couple returned often, told their friends and had their wedding reception there. That maître d's inspiration surprised and delighted the couple.

How many times have you had to attempt to navigate the labyrinth of automated answering services only to be sent back where you started? How many times have you just given up? Well that frustration was the inspiration for Ruby Receptionists.

CEO Jill Nelson had her own stories about the phone service from hell. She compared these to stories of friends and colleagues. Out of this arose Ruby Receptionists.

In business since 2003, Ruby Receptionists aim to return business reception to a time of friendly, cheerful, and professional call answering firs impressions.

Ruby Receptionists answer phones for small business owners who don't have the staff to answer their own phones and want a personal connection to clients and the public. The company has grown from one person in a small sculptor's studio in Portland, Oregon to over a hundred team members in two offices.

There's a reason Ruby Receptionists is a five-time winner of the award for the Fastest Growing Company in Oregon and winner of *Fortune Magazine's* #1 Small Company to Work. Ruby Receptionists deliver what they promise — and then some.

Calls are answered quickly and professionally. Employees are helpful, enthusiastic, and efficient. But beyond that Ruby Receptionists are masters of making "movie moments".

What do I mean? Things like sending homemade cookies to a client who was home with a broken leg or her very own Oscar replica to a client who expressed a wish to attend just one Oscar night. Or express posting doggie biscuits to a client's new puppy. Children and grandchildren of Ruby clients have received cards or small gifts on special occasions. Ruby Receptionists continually surprise and delight clients with unexpected "movie moments".

Moving into a retirement home can be naturally stressful for the individual and the family. When the family finally got mother relocated and settled in they were exhausted, hungry, and too tired to think about food. The owner of the retirement home had dinner ready for the family before they flew home. Her kindness surprised and delighted them and made them instant raving fans.

Stop by the drive-through at Western State Bank in Devils Lake, North Dakota on any Wednesday and you'll find bank tellers outside ready to clean your windshield. On Wild Wednesdays at Western State Bank, the bank employees take half-hour shifts for two hours.

During that time they surprise and delight customers by washing the windshields. They also pass out tickets for door prizes, and bring tasty treats to your car door. More than one potential customer has driven in because he did not believe what his friends had told him. Almost to a person, these people have stayed to open an account and become raving fans.

Every Friday morning, the RBC Branch in Atlanta offers fresh from the oven cookies to its clients and service personnel. The manager bakes these cookies herself. Delivery companies who usually deliver later in the week make it a priority to do deliveries at the RBC branch on Friday mornings!

Boston business HUB Plumbing & Mechanical "surprise and delight" their customers.

When they complete a plumbing job they replace the customer's toilet paper rolls with ones that bear the HUB plumbing logo. It is not costly but it is a "movie moment".

A cleaning company leaves a special Christmas CD in their clients' players during the Christmas season. The CD bears the cleaning company's logo and a special Christmas message.

One employer takes the term "movie moments" to a new level. He shows a movie each month in the company's theatre/meeting room. The occasion includes free popcorn, soft drinks and snacks that fit the locale of the movie. The movies are family friendly. Employees are encouraged to bring family. The nights have spawned pre-movie potluck dinners!

Ways Your Home Healthcare Business Can Surprise and Delight Clients

Handwritten Notes

Take a page from the how to book of the CEO of Headphones.com.

During our first holiday sales season, one way we inspired word-of-mouth support for LSTN Headphones was by writing handwritten notes to each customer who purchased a pair of headphones. It seems simple, but it made a huge difference!

Raise the Bar

Set the standards high. Don't just aim at having satisfied clients. Aim higher. Why? Clients who are merely satisfied don't often share their experiences. Rave reviews come from happy clients. Happy clients are those who have been surprised and delighted by your service. Shock them with delight. Wow them with service.

Bake them Cookies

AppSumo CEO, Noah Kagan, sends his clients amazing cookies completely out of the blue — for no reason! This random, simple gesture means so much to loyal clients. If not cookies then bread or brownies or…

Provide Personal Service

PeoplePerHour has over 500,000 users. They surprise and delight clients with game tickets to see a favorite team or theatre tickets to a show they've been wanting to see. Clients are surprised and amazed that the CEO of the company took time to remember them.

Get to Know Clients as People!

Learn your customers' names and some personal information. Establish a friendship with them because you're trying to meet their needs. Ask about their kids and parents. It's great because you really build a strong relationship with the client.

Value the Little Gestures

From time to time, Unassist sends gifts to clients. It could be a favorite tea or coffee, notepaper, fudge... It's not the cost of the gift. It's the fact that it is specially selected for that client.

Be an Advocate for Your Clients

Real customer advocacy means looking out for your clients' best interest — even if it means a short-term loss for your home healthcare business. Your client may need less of your service or he may need out-of-home care in a hospital or seniors' facility. Advocate for your clients' needs. Show them that their well-being is paramount.

Say Thanks!

Send handwritten thank you cards, or wine, or cheeses, and fruit baskets during the holidays or special moments to show your appreciation for client loyalty.

Use Social Media to Honor Clients

Follow clients' Facebook and other social media accounts. Participate in discussions. Retweet good client tweets.

This shows you are paying attention to them and that you're on the same page. This establishes a bond between you and your clients and respect what they are saying.

Acknowledge Special Moments in Clients' Lives

Provide a gift or a gift card for coffee or lunch or... Your clients will be surprised and excited that you remembered their special day.

Send Postcards

Send handwritten postcards with your business' logo on them to show clients you appreciate them and why. The postcards may contain a fun quote or saying or cartoon.

Remember Shared Milestones

Remember shared milestones: date the company opened, date the client joined your company, a company anniversary… You might have a client party or cake, or a small token gift…

Let Them Know You are Thinking of Them

It's nice for clients to know you were thinking of them. Check in with clients with a phone call or a visit or send articles you know they might enjoy. Do these things between your regular visits and you will create "movie moments" for your clients. You can bet they will tell others!

Chapter Ten: Deliver More Every Time

Don't ever promise more than you can deliver, but always deliver more than you promise.
~Lou Holtz

Ralph Waldo Emerson pessimistically stated: "All promise outruns performance."

It's not the over delivering part that is dangerous. Over delivering and WOW-ing your clients is good business. Delivering more every time increases customer satisfaction. This, in turn, garners repeat business. Word of mouth stories about over delivery creates new referrals.

When you ask potential clients to engage you, you are asking them to make a choice and a costly investment in your home healthcare business.

They are taking a financial risk. By offering careful plans, great references, face-to-face visits you give trust. By doing what you promised — and going beyond those promises you WOW clients and make them raving fans.

You want your clients to understand no request is too much. Companies like Best Buy proved to their clients that no product, no adaptation, no combination was too much of a bother.

As one hotel puts it regarding guest requests: "The answer is yes. The question is how." They promise to grant customer requests. That's a given. Then they set out to make it happen. This hotel has garnered great publicity and raving fans by doing such things as:

- Delivering BBQ ribs from a favourite Chicago restaurant
- Finding a new home for a beloved pet
- Locating and packing toys to amuse a client who had had a fall and couldn't swim

- Getting the autograph of a beloved childhood star
- Acquiring first class tickets to a sold out show
- Arranging a cooking class with the chef

Headsets.com is a good example of over delivering. ON THEIR WEBSITE, THEY SAY THEY HAVE A TWO-HOUR GUARANTEE CALL-BACK TIME FOR CUSTOMER SUPPORT ISSUES. WHEN A CUSTOMER SUBMITS A REQUEST FOR A CALL, THE CUSTOMER EXPECTS A CALL BACK WITHIN 2 HOURS. HEADSETS.COM'S CUSTOMER SUPPORT TEAM IS COMMITTEE TO A RESPONSE WITHIN ONE HOUR. IMAGINE HOW SURPRISED AND DELIGHTED CLIENTS ARE. THIS OVER DELIVER EVEN IMPRESSES DISGRUNTLED CLIENTS!

Another example of WOW-ing customers is Disney Corporation. Disney World makes unbelievable promises to its prospective visitors when you they enter their theme parks. And, not only meet those promises. They over deliver in a big way!

If Disney had listened to traditional business advice they would have offered the bare minimum. Then when they over delivered on their under promising, visitors would be blown away. But, instead, Disney makes big promises and the delivers beyond visitors' wildest expectations. No matter how great the hype, Disney patrons, excited about arriving, are still blown away by their experience. It is little wonder Disney Land has become known as "the happiest place on the earth".

Disney promises are huge. They are far and away bigger and better than their competitors. They promise the moon and over deliver!

How does Disney over deliver? First of all it is one of the cleanest places in the world. Disney Land and Disney World are under constant cleaning by a motivated staff.

Disney personnel are committed to seeing that you have the best time of your life—no matter your age, mobility, culture or language. One senior citizen writes of her many trips to Disney Land:

You can't say enough about Disneyland. I have been there at least 50 times since it opened. I enjoy every single visit and look forward to seeing my favorite places in the park. We always take visitors from out of the area there and it is wonderful to see their enjoyment and surprise at how large it is and how much there is to see and do there. If you only get to see one thing when you visit Southern California, this should be it.

Disney understands about red-carpet treatment for every guest. Visitors of every age are made to feel special. Disney has even made standing in line an entertainment form with magicians, roving Disney characters, buskers, and minstrels.

Everywhere you go in the park you meet Disney staff that makes hello an art.

Disney also understands the art of a good good-bye with waving staff, friendly adieu, parting gifts, and opportunities to tell them what they can do even better!

Disney is not the only company that over delivers. Ruby Receptionists do their jobs efficiently, enthusiastically and with a "can do" attitude that includes surprise gestures for clients and their families. Going the extra mile is all in a day's work for them.

You can learn a lot from other companies' over delivering. Many of the strategies can be applied to your home healthcare business.

The concept of over deliver is simple. Deliver early, on budget, and better than promised. If you promised to have the report finished by Monday, first thing, have it done by then—or earlier. Also add features the client did not expect to receive like the full implementation plans for the new premises.

If you said you'd have the exhibition up and running by Sunday night have it ready by Sunday morning. Or deliver on time while you are short staffed. Create an advertising display that is so amazing it causes your major competitor to pull out of the show. If you promised the first draft of a proposal to a referring doctor or hospital for your company's new brochure by your next meeting have this and a full color mock-up, edited, with photos.

Over delivery means that you will *never* deliver late or deliver short. That's it. If you have to sweat blood and work all night then so be it. You will deliver when you said you would – or earlier – without exception.

It is easy to get caught up in the hype of over delivering. The client's reaction is better than chocolate to create a high.

The caution is: better to negotiate a longer delivery time than to have renege on your promise and disappoint a client.

A lot of people are so keen to be liked, or approved of, or praised that they will agree to a ridiculously tight time line. The result is: they fail. This makes them look incompetent and unreliable. Promise carefully as headphones.com did. They promised a call back within two hours fully planning on a one-hour time limit. The result? They over delivered and WOW-ed their clients.

A brief look at banks reinforces this point. If a bank promises "We'll be back to you." it is a weak promise. Other weak promises include, "Someone will contact you." and "We're referring this matter." Or they say, "We'll get back to you by 3 and it is 4:30 when they finally call."

How much more awesome would it be if they promised to get back by three and called before lunch? That's what over delivering is all about.

Montana's Restaurant promises "quick lunch" specials in fifteen minutes or it's free. Actually they are set up to get these specials to their customers in under ten minutes. This WOWs the hungry clientele on a tight lunch hour and makes them raving fans. Clients rate low even those businesses they like if they fail to deliver when they promised they would. Customers put their faith and business with lower performing businesses that deliver when or sooner than they said they would.

If a hotel promises breakfast service by 6:00 only to have guests waiting at a locked door at 6:15 this is bad for business. How much smarter would it have been to advertise 6:30 breakfast and aim to be open and ready to receive early birds at 6:10? The delay is infuriating when a 6:00 opening was promised. Customers *perceive* they are getting rotten service.

Surprise and delight customers by having the item in stock and at an even cheaper price than advertised. Wal-Mart has built a veritable kingdom on over delivering.

Surgical patients who are told, in detail, about what will occur before, during and after surgery recover as much as one third faster than those who are not prepared for what is to come. This type of over delivery is priceless.

Responsiveness and feedback are the life blood of any business. Despite the quality of your product or service, clients will rate your business on whether you came through on your promises and whether your response was timely.

A tire company that sold excellent tires lost sales because items were not there within the promised time and customers were inconvenienced by having to return.

80 percent of the customer feedback harps on responsiveness and reliability. Quite frequently, companies with lower quality products will gain clients because they unfailingly met their commitments.

Yes, quality is important. But so is response time and promises made and kept. Customers rate highly companies that keep their word. Those companies who realize this and "over deliver" on their promises are the ones that will keep happy customers.

There is ample proof of the power of over delivering. Companies like American Girl, Best Buy, Washington Mutual, and TiVo swept the market in their respective areas. They outsold bigger and wealthier competition because they kept their promises . . .

These weren't just everyday promises. They were dangerously ambitious pledges.

These companies *overpromised* to lure customers. Then they *over delivered* on those promises and got raving fans who became repeat customers=.

Rick Barrera, marketing consultant and keynote speaker, refers to these word-of-mouth-driven successes. He calls this TouchPoint Branding. TouchPoint Branding is simply the art of making sure that every point of contact between a company and its customers is efficient, memorable and gives the customer even more than he expected. In other words: the client is WOW-ed.

According to Barrera, TouchPoint Branding has three major components: Product TouchPoints, System TouchPoints, and Human TouchPoints. When combined these can create dramatic marketing results.

In his book, *Over Promise and Over Deliver: The Secrets of Unshakable Customer Loyalty,* Barrera features companies that have products that over deliver. An example of a product over delivers is   System over delivery examples include: Hummer's smooth running system. Molly Maid is another example of a system that over delivers as is Wal-Mart's online ordering system.

A Human TouchPoints examples cited include Sumerset Houseboats' website and the service at an American Girl store.

It's an old cliché in business that smart companies under promise and over deliver. But in today's crowded market, that's not enough. Barrera's insights and case studies can help any company overpromise . . . and still over deliver.

Here's how you might over deliver on the promises you make to clients of your home healthcare business:

1. Include a handwritten thank you note

Personally handwritten notes are a lost idea in today's digital world. Believe it or not, getting real notes sent through the mail is a cherished occurrence. With just 44 cents and one minute of your time, you can over deliver and create an incredibly happy customer. Surprise and delight your clients by sending them a handwritten note.

2. Personalize Receipts

Jazz up those crappy receipts that are emailed to us. Add a personalized photo from the founder of your company — or his dog as one pet supply company does! Why not try a funny animated GIF. Surprise and delight by including a discount code for their next purchase! Surprise and delight with a creative receipt.

3 Surprise and Delight with an Extra Secret Service or Product

Add an extra product or service your clients are not expecting to receive. If you sell sponsorships for a conference, each sponsor gets booth space, a logo on the website, a logo on the conference name tags, a log on the conference t-shirts, and time on stage to address the audience. Surprise conference attendees by sharing their company on your conference website and email list where you can shout out your sponsors. You don't have to be wildly creative to surprise people. Simply exceed their expectations.

Restaurants over deliver by offering a free appetizer or movie tickets with two dinners on certain week-day nights.

Think about how you can over deliver in your home healthcare business.

4. Provide Random Refunds

Imagine the reaction you'd get if you refunded a client each month or a quarter for a specific service or added an additional free service. This gesture would have little effect on your bottom line. You could offer to refund them, pay their purchase forward to a friend, or donate that money to a charity of their choice.

News of this gesture will go viral! What a great piece of word of mouth marketing. Focus this over delivering on customer retention not on getting new customers!

Your clients want to know the exact services they are getting. They also want to be convinced of tangible benefits. Save one or two benefits for later. That way you can build a "wow" factor with extra perks. Your happy clients will become raving fans.

Plan ahead to surprise and delight clients! Sometimes these things occur spontaneously like the ice cream delivered on a hot day. Often the best examples of over delivering are part of a carefully thought out marketing plan.

Helpful Resources

Barrera, Rick. (2004) *Over Promise and Over Deliver: The Secrets of Unshakable Customer Loyalty.* http://www.amazon.com/Overpromise-Overdeliver-Secrets-Unshakable-Customer/dp/B000BOB30Q

Books, Lorenz (1999) *601 Do-It-Yourself Marketing Ideas from America's Most Innovative Small Companies.* http://www.amazon.com/301-Do-It-Yourself-Marketing-Ideas-Innovative/ dp/1880394308/ref=pd_sim_b_6?ie=UTF8&refRID=0 GW5JTKGQ1X89YVR8DPT

Cialdini, Robert. *Influence: The Psychology of Persuasion. http://www.amazon.com/Influence-Psychology-Persuasion-Revised-Edition/dp/006124189X*

Cutting, Donna. *The Celebrity Experience: Insider Secrets to Delivering Red Carpet Customer Service.*

http://www.amazon.com/Celebrity-Experience-
Insider-Delivering-
Customer/dp/0470174013/ref=sr_1_1?s=books&ie=
UTF8&qid=1426526676&sr=1-
1&keywords=donna+cutting
Cutting, Donna (2015) *501 Ways to Roll out the Red
Carpet for Your Customers*
Edwards, Paul and Edwards, Sarah (1998). *Getting
Business to Come to You.*
*http://www.amazon.com/Getting-Business-To-Come-
You/dp/087477845X*

Ellenbecker, C. et al., "Patient Safety and Quality in
Home Health Care".
http://www.ncbi.nlm.nih.gov/books/NBK2631/

Entrepreneur. "10 Laws of Social Media Marketing"
http://www.entrepreneur.com/article/218160

Frey, David. How to Make it Rain Referrals.
http://www-
rohan.sdsu.edu/~renglish/377/notes/chapt07/raini
ng_referra.htm

Gerber, Scott. "Marketing Mistakes that Make You
Look Like a Rookie".
http://mashable.com/2014/12/04/rookie-
marketing-mistakes/

Haden, Jeff. *The 9 Elements of Highly Effective Employee
Praise*

Healthcare Associates. "12 Critical Questions to
Evaluate before Hiring a Homecare Agency"
http://healthcareassociates.net/12-critical-
characteristics-to-evaluate-before-hiring-a-home-care-
agency/

"Marketing Your Business to Consumers"
http://www.homecarepulse.com/articles/marketing
-business-consumers-start/
National Health Statistics Report #52, April, 2012.
http://www.cdc.gov/nchs/data/nhsr/nhsr052.pdf

Pinskey, Walter (1999) *101 Ways to Promote Yourself.*
http://www.amazon.com/101-Ways-Promote-
Yourself-
Success/dp/0380810549/ref=pd_sim_b_6?ie=UTF8&r
efRID=1PSCZGJ0SS7K6K4DCDFQ

Red Carpet.com. "Let us Show You the Red-Carpet
Treatment". http://redcarpettreatment.org/

Robertson, Bobbie. "Using Marketing to Increase
Referrals for Home Care Agencies" in *Home Healthcare
and Hospice Industry Blog.*
http://blog.healthcarefirst.com/bid/30585/Using-
Marketing-to-Increase-Referrals-for-Home-Care-
Agencies
"The 6 Habits of Highly Effective Marketers: Cracking
the Code of Internet Marketing Strategies"
http://www.designdamage.com/the-6-habits-of-
highly-effective-marketers/#ixzz3UZCN7nDJ

"What not to do when Using Social Media for Business".
http://sbinformation.about.com/od/marketingsales /a/what-not-to-do-when-using-social-media-for-business.htm

www.ingramcontent.com/pod-product-compliance
Lightning Source LLC
Chambersburg PA
CBHW070855180526
45168CB00005B/1832